About Play England

Play England is the national campaigning, support and development agency for children's play and play provision. Play England promotes excellent free play opportunities for all children and young people. It provides advice and support to promote good practice, and works to ensure that the importance of play is recognised by policy-makers, planners and the public.

Play England is part of the National Children's Bureau, and is supported by the Big Lottery Fund.

Play England

Making space for play

Supported by
The National Lottery®
through the Big Lottery Fund

BIG
LOTTERY
FUND

First published in 2007
© Play England
Some rights reserved
See copyright licence for details

ISBN 1 84180 188 7
Copy edited by Julie Pickard, London
Designed and printed by Divamedia, Bristol
www.divamedia.co.uk

For further information and subscription details please contact:

Demos
Third Floor
Magdalen House
136 Tooley Street
London SE1 2TU

Telephone: 020 7367 4200
email: hello@demos.co.uk
web: www.demos.co.uk

Seen and Heard

Reclaiming the public realm with children and young people

Joost Beunderman
Celia Hannon
Peter Bradwell

DEM⊙S

Contents

Acknowledgements

This report was commissioned by and would not have been possible without the support of Play England, part of the National Children's Bureau (NCB). Issy Cole-Hamilton and Adrian Voce of Play England provided us with advice and guidance throughout the project. Many thanks, also, to Becky McLauchlan of Play England and Anna Kassman-McKerrell at NCB's Children's Play Information Service for their input and assistance at different stages of the project.

We are very grateful to Melissa Mean and Hannah Green for their invaluable input and reflections at every stage of the research and writing process.

We would like to thank Jane Leighton, Leila Baker and Nick Edwards from Fundamental Architectural Inclusion for their input into the case study research for this project, and Ann Clare for additional fieldwork. They were excellent collaborators on this part of the project; the case studies would not have been possible without their intelligence, thoroughness and organisational talent.

At Demos our thanks go to all the interns who helped with the research, events and organisation of the project: particularly Amy Horton, Miranda Kimball, Morgan Saxby and Poppy Nicol. We would also like to thank Alessandra Buonfino who commented on the draft and supported our efforts in the final stages of the project. Peter Harrington guided the pamphlet through to publication; he, Victoria Shooter and Mark Fuller helped us at various stages to communicate our ideas.

We are indebted to many individuals who contributed to our work through participating in interviews, speaking at seminars and offering advice. Special thanks go to Tim Gill and Helen Woolley for their helpful and insightful comments throughout the research.

Thanks should also go to the local place-shaping professionals who gave their valuable time to participate in, as well as often helping to organise, our case studies. Finally, we would like to thank the many children and young people who spent time talking to us, guiding us through their local environments and giving us invaluable and honest insights into their everyday experiences in the public realm.

As always, all errors and omissions remain our own.

Joost Beunderman
Celia Hannon
Peter Bradwell
September 2007

Foreword

by Adrian Voce

Some things are self-evident. One is that children need space to play.

That is, the specific, measurable outcomes of children playing can be researched, evaluated and debated, and will undoubtedly need to be (more than they have already) in order to provide the reliable evidence base that is the prerequisite of policy development. So, too, the extent and the type of space that best (and most cost-effectively) provides for this need for children in different circumstances needs to be studied and analysed.

But no one who has children, works with children or can remember being a child questions that play is intrinsic to a good childhood, and that playing needs some space. Almost by definition, children denied space to play are repressed.

Ironically, the quintessential nature of play has been one of the problems in getting it taken seriously as a policy issue. It seems that play is conceived as so inseparable from childhood itself that the adult population in the main, and policy-makers in particular, have simply taken it for granted. In a world that values children mainly as 'the future', this thing that they do for themselves now seems less important than training and equipping them for later in life.

Nevertheless, accumulating evidence from a range of academic and media commentators has given rise to a growing concern across the political spectrum that the creeping infringement into space and time that was traditionally children's own is causing real and potential harm.

For nearly 20 years, the Children's Play Council (CPC), an alliance of like-minded organisations led by the National Children's Bureau, has campaigned to promote children's play. It has researched and highlighted the steady decline in play opportunities in England and worked with many colleague organisations across all sectors to formulate a policy agenda to address the need for more and better play provision and play space for all children.

Underpinning this work has always been the recognition that, as a human right under the United Nations Convention on the Rights of the Child, the provision for children's play should not be left to the market, but should be seen as part of policy-making for the public realm. CPC's position is that, whatever the market may provide, children's essential, everyday play needs should be met by the planning and design of accessible, playable public space wherever children live. In addition, freely available supervised play services – staffed adventure playgrounds, for example – should be provided where the concentration of children and the premium on space demands it.

Children will always flock to the fairground and theme park, and enjoy soft play areas in shopping centres and the like, as long as their families can afford the entry fee. But the provision for children's need to play should not be conceived as equivalent to the adult leisure industry. This is partly because children are not independent consumers and partly because play is more fundamentally important for children than leisure activities are for adults. For children, the opportunity to play is their equivalent to our freedom of movement, freedom of association, freedom of expression. Without regular time, space and permission to play, children are denied the right to be themselves, to follow their own unique agenda. The consequences for their quality of life, health and development – and, by extension, their future life chances too – are serious.

When CPC was asked by the Big Lottery Fund in 2005 to form Play England to help it to shape and support its new Children's Play Initiative, one of our main discussions was about how the initiative should be strategic. We wanted the initiative to promote change across the whole landscape of policy and practice areas that impact on the places and spaces where children might play. More and better local children's playgrounds, and some good, inclusive supervised play projects like adventure playgrounds, are, for many areas, going to be the best use of a relatively modest allocation of funds. But the focusing of minds on producing local play strategies that address the broader question of a 'playable' public realm and how to sustain cross-cutting improvements would give the initiative a chance to have a longer-term and more profound impact.

Nationally, too, we proposed that resources be directed to researching the evidence base, exploring the policy issues and making the case for the shift in government policy. We saw this as necessary in driving a long-term change in the priority given to children's needs in the planning and design of environments.

Hence, Play England, awarded £15 million over five years as part of the initiative, was able, in 2006, to commission Demos to conduct this study of children's relationship with the public realm. We think the study is thorough and the analysis thought provoking. We hope that it stimulates debate and challenges policy-makers, planners and practitioners to take children's need for space to play – and young people's need for space to socialise and live their own cultural and recreational lives – more seriously.

We hope that it adds further weight to the growing movement for a cultural shift in how our society perceives and responds to its children and young people. Central to that movement is the simple recognition that children need space to play, and that it is up to us to provide it.

Ultimately, we hope that this report takes us a step closer to a society where children really are at the heart of their communities, not just rhetorically, but physically, spatially: out, playing, where they belong.

Adrian Voce is Director of
Play England

Introduction

At the time of writing this introduction the twentieth annual Playday has just taken place. The day is designed to celebrate the right of children to play outside. This year's theme – *Our streets too!* – highlights how children want and need to play in their local streets and have a legitimate right to be there.

A survey commissioned by Play England for Playday reveals how under threat this right is. Among those polled, 71 per cent of adults played outside in the street or area close to their homes every day when they were children whereas only 21 per cent of children do so today.[1]

This stark statistic does not stand alone. Recent years have seen a remarkable rise in the attention paid to the issues of children and young people in public space. Media headlines, research reports, policy statements and, indeed, young people's own voices convey a strong message that all is not well.

Media headlines from the last year have declared that the UK's teenagers are the worst behaved in Europe,[2] that childhood is now considered 'toxic',[3] and that 'Britain has lost the art of socialising the young'.[4]

These flares of alarm are given substance by a growing number of weighty policy reports. The charity 4Children warns that 'school holiday misery looms for millions of teenagers'.[5] The chair of the Commons Public Accounts Committee (PAC) spoke out claiming that 'drunken yobs' were turning town centres into no-go areas, and that anti-social youngsters were 'behaving like an occupying army' and bringing 'misery and despair' to communities.[6] Perhaps most damningly, the UK drew heavy criticism in a report by Unicef, which placed Britain at the bottom of 21 developed countries in a league table of children's wellbeing.[7] Responding to its findings Al Aynsley-Green, the Children's Commissioner, said: 'We are turning out a generation of young people who are unhappy, unhealthy, engaging in risky behaviour, who have poor relationships with their family and their peers, who have low expectations and don't feel safe.'[8]

The heightened anxiety comes during a period in which, arguably, government has been very ambitious in seeking to improve children's lives with a remarkable number of new initiatives and high-profile statements of intent. This Labour government has introduced a Minister for Children, Young People and Families; Children's Commissioners for Northern Ireland, Wales, Scotland and England; and now families have their own government department and cabinet post as part of the new Department for Children, Schools and Families. At the same time the 2004 Children Act and the Every Child Matters agenda, along with its companion for young people, Youth Matters, seeks to put children's and young people's wellbeing at the heart of a reformed system of public service delivery.

With all this effort some success has been achieved. The number of children living in poverty is falling, overall educational achievement is improving and key indicators for teenagers, such as smoking, under-18 conception rates and drug use, show a decline.[9]

Moreover, fine words[10] have been accompanied by some resources for play too. For example, Play England itself was established in 2006, with a five-year remit to promote strategies for free play and to create a lasting support structure for play providers in England, as part of the Big Lottery Fund's £155 million Children's Play initiative to encourage free, mainly outdoor, play opportunities.[11]

However, there remains a significant gap between these improvements in the lives of individual children and young people and wider public perceptions of how children and young people are faring in general. This pamphlet argues that one important reason for this gap is that until now action to improve the lives of children and young people has tended to focus on the institutional spheres of home and school and individualised approaches to improving quality of life. While such an approach has value it also has its limitations.

For quality of life is not just about individual success. It also depends on the quality of and access to shared resources – in other words the health of the public realm. And here children and young people suffer from a mix of invisibility, segregation and exclusion. They are, for example, invisible in economically dominated town centre regeneration strategies which prioritise commercial interests and uses; they are segregated spatially, temporally and by age into designated play areas and supervised activities; and finally, they face exclusion from public spaces and places through a combination of adult fears and complaints, legal controls and dispersal orders, and even high-tech tricks such as the infamous 'sonic teenage deterrent', the Mosquito.[12]

At a time when investment and interest in the public realm is at a historical high under the tag of the urban renaissance, children and young people are simply not part of the script. For example, one study found that fewer than one in five (17 per cent) young people thought that their area cares about its young people and almost half reported that there are no places for young people to go in their neighbourhood.[13]

The research undertaken for this report across six different neighbourhoods suggests that the government's ambitions to improve the wellbeing of children, and its aim to create sustainable communities, will fall short unless the needs of children and young people in their everyday environment are taken seriously by all those designing, delivering and managing the public realm in its broadest sense.

This pamphlet also shows where this is already happening. Across the country, children and adults are engaged in improving playgrounds, parks and streets to make them more welcoming to children and young people. All

This pamphlet

of the case studies, despite their often challenging circumstances and starting positions, have some part of the story right, and in that sense this pamphlet is a story of hope.

However, such good practices will fall flat unless our cities, towns and neighbourhoods come to terms with the fact that children and young people have the right to be seen and heard in public: to play, socialise and, above all, to be themselves. The prize lies not just in terms of improving the individual lot of children and young people, but also in making better, more imaginative, more human cities, towns and neighbourhoods.

This pamphlet is divided into three sections, containing six chapters overall:

Part One: Making the case
Chapter 1 gives an overview of the benefits of a good public realm. It introduces a broad conception of public space, its diversity, its benefits to children and how such benefits are related to wider society.

Chapter 2 outlines how the promise of the public realm contrasts with the reality of children's experience in their everyday built environment. This chapter outlines the *symptoms* of what has become a dysfunctional relationship between children and young people and public space.

Part Two: Spaces, stories and shaping places
Chapter 3 shows how some of the problems that children experience are part of a wider set of pressures impacting on the quality of the built environment. These pressures include increased building

densities, the dominance of the car, and the spatial segmentation of towns and cities into different functions.

Chapter 4 shows how the decline in children's places in public is not just a *spatial* issue, but is also socially constituted: cultural attitudes to childhood and to children and young people actively restrict where children can go and what they can do. This chapter investigates the tension between the fear *for* children and the fear *of* children and young people, arguing that both narratives have combined to diminish children's freedom in public space.

Chapter 5 explores how the task of improving the public realm for children and young people is hampered by a lack of awareness about how the decisions made by professionals when delivering spaces impact on children. This chapter looks at some of the barriers to better practice faced by professionals such as planners, town centre managers or highways officers.

Part Three: Where next?
Chapter 6 concludes by proposing a series of practical actions and first steps to realise the potential of shared spaces, for children and young people and for everyone who uses and inhabits the public realm.

Methodology

Demos was commissioned by Play England to investigate the social and physical limits on children's access to the public realm, and to address the wider social, cultural and political context in which it is being shaped. This pamphlet is the outcome of a nine-month investigation into the experiences of children and young people in the public realm along with research into the role of professionals in shaping those experiences.

The research for this report began with an initial stage of background research, drawing on existing academic literature, statistical data and policy documents. The subsequent methodology, approach and research questions were tested at a joint Demos / Play England seminar in January 2007, which brought together senior policy-makers, academics, public space experts and practitioners from the play and urban design sector. The seminar and a series of expert interviews preceding and following it provided invaluable feedback on our early findings and suggestions for further research (see Appendix 1).

Over the next four months Demos undertook a series of six case studies across the UK to investigate children's and young people's everyday experiences in the public realm, as well as speaking to a large and diverse group of adults who are professionally involved in creating, maintaining and managing elements of the public realm – the 'place-shapers'. More information on the range of professionals interviewed can be found in Appendix 2.

Finally, in May 2007 Demos convened a group of senior place-making professionals from a wide variety of backgrounds at a 'place-shapers forum'. The aim of the forum was to discuss the case study findings and local analysis, and connect them to nationwide challenges in policy-making for children and young people in the public realm.

The six case study locations were the Upper Horfield estate in Bristol, West View in Fleetwood, the town centres of Sheffield and Maidstone, Heywood Park in Bolton and Spa Fields in Islington, London. We worked together with researchers from Fundamental Architectural Inclusion, based in Newham, London, to speak to more than 60 children and young people about their local environment – about what possibilities their local public spaces gave them to play, about their desires and needs, the obstacles they perceive, the worries they have and their ideas for improvement.

The children were aged between six and 18 and they showed the research team around their localities on walking trips, marking information on local maps and in reporting booklets, as well as describing their experiences in group discussions, individual interviews and through interviewing each other*.

The case studies were not designed to cover the full range of places in which children and young people experience the public realm. The aim was to start with the children and identify the spaces and places that were important to them. These incorporated a diversity of localities with mixed demographic and spatial conditions, but it must be recognised that they do not form a comprehensive account of all possible types of spaces, particularly in rural locations.

* throughout the pamphlet, all names of children and young people have been changed to ensure anonymity

Part One
Making the case

01. The promise of the public realm to children and young people

The young of all creatures cannot be quiet in their bodies or in their voices; they are always wanting to move and cry out; some leaping and skipping, and overflowing with sportiveness and delight at something.

Plato[14]

States Parties recognize the right of the child to rest and leisure, to engage in play and recreational activities appropriate to the age of the child and to participate freely in cultural life and the arts.

Article 31 of the UN Convention on the Rights of the Child[15]

Children's play has always been a powerful agent of social and cultural change. Yet, frankly, until relatively recently it has been a secret agent, undervalued by politicians and policy makers alike. . . play is so central to what we need to achieve across Government: (reducing) obesity; better public space; safer streets; the respect agenda. . .

David Lammy, Minister for Culture, 2006[16]

The public realm

The freedom of children and young people to roam around, to play independently and to discover the world is crucial to their development and happiness. Much of this happens in the private domain such as the home and other family situations, or in institutional settings like the school or the sports club. A significant portion, however, takes place in public spaces – from the foraging adventures of a day in the park to a simple walk to school. Because of the importance of this process of discovery and development, the way that children experience the public realm, and how they are treated in it, is an integral part of their wellbeing.

The benefits of a good public realm for children and young people are part of the benefits it gives the rest of society. When it functions well, public space is a free shared resource for all to draw on, a realm for everyday sociability, and a safe setting for face-to-face interaction between strangers.

Although often associated with great civic squares and boulevards, public space is also about the small and the informal, encompassing a diverse range of spaces, such as streets and pavements, parks, community gardens, allotments – even cul-de-sacs. A healthy public realm can support an equally diverse range of activities – from mass political demonstrations, to the most mundane activities such as waiting for a bus in comfort, or watching the world go by. Indeed, the very vitality of a public space depends on how it responds to the widest range of people's needs, desires and aspirations, and how it facilitates people's creativity and imagination to engage with it.

In plural, democratic societies, the public realm, more than anything else, manifests what Doreen Massey has called our 'throwntogetherness', providing touchpoints from which trust can develop across the diversity in our cities and towns.[17] The value of a well-functioning public realm lies primarily in its potential to create these bonds between citizens, across social cleavages, enabling relevant links with public institutions and community resources. This is why the public realm is so important to people's wellbeing: as a shared resource, it can sustain and improve people's quality of life, providing the setting for new experiences, human exchange and the creation of value in ways that are not possible in people's private lives alone. Far from being something prescribed by policy-makers and urban academics, everyone cares about the public space around them. In a recent study, 85 per cent of people polled even said that the quality of public space has a direct impact on their lives and the way they feel.[18]

Public space, then, can offer something of a barometer of the state of social relations – within an individual neighbourhood and society overall – by revealing how people relate, and are expected to relate, to each other. This pamphlet maps how children are currently treated and what role they are permitted to play in the public realm. It explores the potential for a better relationship between children and place, and between children and other people. The prize lies not just in creating a public realm that can more fully support the wellbeing of children, but in creating places that are better for everyone.

Children, young people and the public realm

Children in cities need a variety of places in which to play and to learn. They need, among other things, opportunities for all kinds of sports and exercise and physical skills. . . However, at the same time, they need an unspecialized outdoor home base from which to play, to hang around in, and to help form their notions of the world.

Jane Jacobs[19]

With limited independence – both financial and in terms of transport – children and young people depend on the public realm more than other groups. Alongside home and school, public spaces and places are the mainstay of children's everyday lives. Crucially, the public realm is one of the arenas for children and young people to engage in the defining elements of youth: it is where they play.

Play can happen in the traditional setting of the playground. But, play means more than swings and slides. It is better defined as 'activities which children choose to undertake when not being told what to do by others'.[20] In other words, it is what children do every day, alone or with friends, and in informal – yet often complex – games. Play involves in-between activities and in-between places, as well as structured activities in designated locations. It is central to a child's healthy development, but at the same time it is not something that can be instrumentalised or rationalised – it is not the behaviour characteristic of the purposeful adult.

As play is about learning the opportunities, limits and games of our social lives, some of the places play happens can be very public – from parks to shopping malls. Interaction with adults can be a crucial part of this; they offer safety, caution, encouragement and, on occasion, admonishment. But equally, places that are away from the gaze of adults take on great importance in a child's life world, such as the local woods, dens and hideaways discovered and constructed in neglected or secret places with friends or alone.

What is important across all these spaces is the sense of agency that spaces and places afford children and young people. Can they help shape them and adapt them for their own purposes? For example, the formal garden turned into a football pitch; guardrails into a landscape for skateboarding; tree trunks into a stage set for a play. This adaptability of the public realm to children's different and changing needs is a critical part of its quality and ability to facilitate a range of experiences and possibilities which in turn are important factors shaping and supporting children's quality of life. As a 2003 Demos report argues: 'Quality of life is not just about individual success. It all depends on the quality of shared resources, or the "commons", on which children rely.'[21]

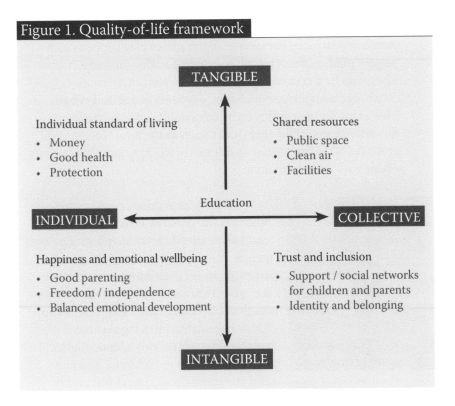

Figure 1. Quality-of-life framework

TANGIBLE

Individual standard of living
• Money
• Good health
• Protection

Shared resources
• Public space
• Clean air
• Facilities

Education

INDIVIDUAL ← → **COLLECTIVE**

Happiness and emotional wellbeing
• Good parenting
• Freedom / independence
• Balanced emotional development

Trust and inclusion
• Support / social networks for children and parents
• Identity and belonging

INTANGIBLE

Source: G Thomas and G Hocking, *Other People's Children: Why their quality of life is our concern* (London: Demos, 2003).

The rest of this chapter focuses on the specific benefits of a healthy and accessible public realm for children. Figure 1 offers a guiding hand in showing how quality of life for children and young people depends on a range of factors, some of which are tangible and readily measurable, some of which are less so. What will become clear is how the benefits of a healthy public realm are multiple, cutting across the individual and the collective interest. Good public spaces for children tend to:

• support active lifestyles
• support personal development and emotional wellbeing
• facilitate learning about wider society

- encourage positive attitudes to nature and sustainable development
- foster citizenship and participation in decision-making.

The final section highlights why it is not just individual children who benefit from a healthy public realm – there are collective benefits for the wider community too.

Health

The public realm is a place where children can be physically active. Given the chance, children are naturally active and will run around, hide, seek, hop and skip wherever they can. Children and young people are said to need at least 60 minutes of medium-intensity physical activity each day.[22] Research shows that play and informal recreation is one of the most effective ways to meet this target for children. One recent study found that unstructured play ranked second in terms of calorific intensity and concluded that 'walking and playing provide children with more physical activity than most other activities'.[23]

Unlike sport, play does not require significant levels of skill and is less centred on competition and winning.

Child development and mental health

Play performs a significant role in child development and mental health. From their very early years, children use play to explore the most fundamental concepts of self, other and the world around them. Their learning takes place through an incredible diversity in situations and experiences, through exploring different materials, developing different bodily skills, learning how to be attentive, expressing emotions and experiencing people's reactions.[24]

Through this process, a healthy child will move from support to independence, and while learning basic skills such as language and literary skills. They also learn to be creative and flexible, negotiate risk and build self-esteem, develop a notion of identity, and develop confidence and a sense of responsibility, as well as their interests in particular aspects of the world outside.[25]

Through children's and young people's active engagement with the physical environment and people around them, play and learning can be seen as inseparably together, with the built environment outside the home taking on increased importance as children grow in age.

Social learning

The process of learning happens in the creative tension between autonomy and connectedness and is embedded in the idea of play as children choosing what they want to do, how they want to do it and when to stop and try something else. As opposed to more formal settings for education, play has little or no adult-defined curriculum or goals.

The process is deeply social, as children learn from and with not just their formal guardians – parents, carers and teachers – but also with their peers and others in society. In the words of *Planning for Play*, 'much of children's play is likely to be spontaneous and unpredictable, although there is a place for more structured activities too where children choose them'; adults' role should be to 'enable, not direct'.[26]

The forging and maintenance of social relationships often involves debate, conflict and negotiation, a degree of which should be accepted and encouraged as part of the learning process.[27] However, it can also be marked by bullying, and the difficult discovery of prejudice and social divisions. Children in vulnerable groups such as those with disabilities or from minority ethnic backgrounds can experience these in particularly negative ways.

Part of the value of the public realm lies in the everyday sociability that takes place here, in which we can learn to live with others through seeing different norms and ways of behaving. Richard Sennett sees the value of the public realm as being a 'place in which strangers can meet in safety', which is secure enough for people to take the risk of engaging with the unfamiliar.[28] Play also provides an important context in which children can counter the effects of poverty and deprivation, through potentially stimulating and welcoming environments. It provides a setting in which children from different backgrounds can interact on equal terms.[29]

Children's agency in the built environment

As children and young people explore the outside world, they often build intimate relationships with the places that surround them. They develop detailed knowledge, often intertwining their own identity with that of the places they spend time in. This active relationship between children and young people and places provides an important foundation for seeing children not merely as objects of adults' care and protection, but rather as citizens with a feeling of ownership and belonging with an active stake in a locality.[30]

For example, environmental campaigners argue that good green spaces do not just have positive psychological effects and evident health benefits in countering the impacts of pollution. There is also a lasting and important link between young people's experiences and perceptions of their environment, and the attitudes they develop towards it.[31] As such, play in the local environment enables children to 'develop the habits and commitments that will enable them to address environmental problems in the future'.[32]

Speaking generally, Ken Worpole and Katherine Knox

remark that 'the success of a particular public space is not solely
in the hands of the architect, urban designer or town planner;
it relies also on people adopting, using and managing the space
– people make places, more than places make people'.[33] This is
equally true for children – in countless informal and formal
ways, children are part of what creates places. In *The Child in
the City*,[34] Colin Ward sketches his ideal of encouraging full
integration of children into community affairs so that adults and
children alike live compatibly in a shared city. Often, children
are an insightful resource for understanding neighbourhood and
community issues, and there are clear benefits for tapping into
such knowledge.

For children and young people, learning the game of
participation in the world's affairs and about the importance
of democratic responsibility occurs only through practical
participation. Involving children and young people actively in
decision-making roles can benefit the local environment as well
as strengthen children's sense of belonging to a locality and also
be an important step towards developing competent participating
citizens.

Wider community benefits

Just as there are benefits of drawing on young people's local
knowledge, there are wider benefits that radiate from a good
public realm for children to the wider community. Contrary
to what is suggested by the dominant media discourse, place
quality for children and place quality for the rest of society are
not opposed. A space that is good for children will often be
good for adults too. Among the benefits of such a space are the
potential to grow local social contacts and trust, to integrate
disparate generations and communities, and to grow participative
neighbourhood processes more generally. Additionally, a public
realm that is healthy for children could help counter some of the

negative behaviours that surveys consistently show people are concerned about, as well as meeting a deeper and largely unmet need in society, namely for playful behaviour beyond the years of childhood and adolescence.

A clear example emerges out of research by Donald Appleyard, a researcher at the University of California, Berkeley, who investigated the social contact between people living on three streets with different levels of car traffic intensity – one of the main detractors from quality public space for children.[35] The research showed that the neighbourliness on less trafficked streets was significantly higher. Research for the Joseph Rowntree Foundation, which evaluated an intergenerational initiative in which people from different neighbourhoods collaboratively debated play and public space, came to a similar conclusion. While working together, divisions between different generations were broken down and understanding grew.[36] This is an important outcome in contemporary Britain, where successive social value surveys show that trust in society is generally (though not always locally) in decline,[37] where attitudes to children are frequently negative, and where intergenerational contact is exceptionally low.[38]

Moreover, the same JRF research found additional benefits of the process. Participants reported that their confidence in their contacts within the neighbourhood and with policy-makers had grown significantly, citing newly learned skills and self-esteem. In other words, the citizenship learning processes that benefit children are not irrelevant to the wider community.[39]

Playful places

Increasingly it is recognised that the distinction between children's playful behaviour and 'serious' adult behaviour is a false one, imprinted in society's consciousness in ways that are damaging to adult health. Brian Sutton-Smith, the dean of Play Studies at the University of Pennsylvania, argues that 'the opposite of play isn't work. It's depression. To play is to act out and be wilful, exultant and committed, as if one is assured of one's prospects.'[40] The cultural historian Johan Huizinga, who coined the term 'Homo Ludens', similarly argued that playful behaviour is key to human culture – play is not just mindless entertainment, but an essential way of dealing with the world and with others, from seemingly aimless wanderings through the city to the rituals of love and friendship.[41]

As writer and social commentator Pat Kane says: 'This is "play" as the great philosophers understood it: the experience of being an active, creative and fully autonomous person.'[42] In contemporary societies, which value creativity as a crucial underpinning of the economy, and in which leisure time and self-realisation are more widely available to most than ever before, such considerations are increasingly powerful.[43] Public spaces that are adaptable, that provide inspiration and stimulus for exploration, games and other non-regulated behaviour, therefore become even more important to sustain the needs of society at large.

Public spaces have always been at the core of the debate of what a good society offers to its citizens. The question of whether we can make the cities, towns and villages we want has always been the subject of intense debate among those thinking about the built environment. Normative visions of what constitutes a 'good city' or 'good town' guide the large and small interventions in the spaces we use everyday – and we need to continually reflect on them to understand our places as they are, and imagine them as they could be.

At different times, children have explicitly been put at the heart of such an imagination – for example in Amsterdam in the late 1940s and 1950s, when the architect Aldo van Eijk questioned assumptions about the functionalist 'machine' cities proposed by his Modernist peers, and created a dense network of play spaces in leftover spaces across the city.[44] Or more recently, when in Bogotá, the conflict-ridden and polluted capital of Colombia, the city embarked on an ambitious series of projects for parks, public transport and children's play spaces, putting them symbolically in prominent spaces in the city as well as dotted around neighbourhoods. When asked about his policies, Enrique Penalosa, mayor of Bogotá, famously said that 'if we can build a successful city for children, we will have a successful city for everyone'.[45]

02. The everyday
reality

A lot of people are getting in trouble – cos there's nowhere to go. . .
they're hanging around on the street. . . and they're like making their
neighbours mad cos there's too much noise. . . we've got nothing to
do round here. . . there's gangs of kids on the street all the time.

Hannah, 17, West View estate, Fleetwood

Hannah is making a point which is specific to her own
neighbourhood but her experience resonates with young people
around the country. When places let young people down, it
impacts directly on their behaviour, and by extension on the
experience of other users who share the space. A dysfunctional
public realm displays a range of symptoms and this chapter
will explore how children experience those symptoms in their
everyday lives.

Hannah lives in a ward which is among the top 10 per cent
most deprived in the UK. There is high unemployment following
the closures of the local fishing industry and petrochemical
plant, and the area is isolated geographically. Speaking about
the provision for children and young people on the estate,
one professional admitted that in many areas 'it just isn't good

enough.[46] There are long-running problems with litter, graffiti and anti-social behaviour, and many of the neighbours in West View at times feel frustrated or threatened by the presence of children on the street.

Such fears and frustrations from children and adults are the reality in many places in Britain today. The research undertaken for this pamphlet reveals children are repeatedly let down by the places they live in. For different reasons, and in different ways, children and young people experience the negative impacts of a public realm that is neglected, unwelcoming, unsafe or downright hostile.

In the short term their self-esteem is undermined by unwelcoming and uncared-for places, creating feelings of powerlessness and disrespect. In the longer term, by inhibiting the freedom to explore the cities, towns and neighbourhoods they live in, it endangers children and young people's health and their socialisation into wider society.

What children and young people told us

The estate

Interviewer   How would you describe this place?

Mandy   When we're having people visiting like you it makes you feel like it's not a very nice place.

Abbie   It's a horrible feeling that people chuck stuff. I mean it's only about two quid to take it to the tip.

Interviewer   What do you think of all the streets with the litter on?

Ben   Disgraceful.

Interviewer   What would you do to help out?

Nick   Clean up the mess. Keep it all nice.

Like many postwar social housing estates, the West View estate has ample open space. However, most of it is run down. Across the country, the open spaces of housing estates are often not considered to constitute public space as such, and therefore they receive less attention than other public spaces. Yet they are hugely important to local children and young people, who experience the consequences of the decline on their doorstep. This frequently compounds other problems that are concentrated on social housing estates, such as deprivation and ill health. Later in the report we will see how the residents of West View tackled the poverty of their shared space, starting with their collective recognition that the local environment was shaping children's behaviour and impacting on their wellbeing.

The park

Deepah   It's a good place to be, but it's dirty.

Jenny   It needs washing.

Gareth   There was this thing where you could slide from one side to the other that was really cool. . . but they burnt it last year and now you can't go any more. And there was also this big sandcastle place. But they took that away.

Dan   I don't like this bin. It's been burnt, it's sharp.

We visited Heywood Park in Bolton, a run-down space which still played an important part of many children's lives in the area. As is often the case, the children there were among the fiercest critics of littering and run-down facilities. In Heywood they particularly worried about its state of repair and the constant vandalism.

The town centre

In Sheffield, the Peace Gardens would seem to provide a rare good example of a space that can be shared by families, young children and teenagers. But positive physical space does not always translate into positive experiences for young people. From one group we met we heard how often they found themselves being moved on by city centre staff, regarded as suspect or made to feel unwelcome – simply for gathering in groups.

Robin They should look at it in a positive way instead of negatively.

Lewis Everybody is different and I think they should look more into that and not just oh cos you're a teenager.

Interviewer How might that work?

Erin Talk to them. Stuff that we've been doing that's in the newspaper, they could look at that.

Lewis They could see we are quite mature.

Youth worker Could invite them to something, to come to a presentation. . .

Ryan I don't think they'd be interested really cos they've already made up their mind.

Ruby Maybe they should be made to go on training. We could deliver the training.

Lewis They could come over and talk to us and find out what we're doing before getting us to move on.

The street

A newly designed residential street in Bristol should also be providing children with a range of opportunities for play and socialising. Instead they are afraid of cars, and many find their streets barren and uninspiring:

Tim　I hate the cars cos they come flying around the corner.

Debby　There is nothing to do here cos they took away the bench.

Tim　All the cars parked around here should be in the private car parks but they don't bother because they're too lazy.

Interviewer　If there weren't any cars here what would this space be good for?

Tim　For football.

(many agree)

Katie　I think this street is boring, I mean nothing's happening.

Debbie　It's a lot of concrete.

The everyday disappointment

As we see in these examples taken from our case studies, too often the opportunities afforded to us by public space are lost to cars, litter or restrictions on freedom. It is these everyday experiences that affect children. Crucially, this has consequences not only for adults' and young people's experiences of the place around them, but for the relationships *between* adults and young people.

In *No Particular Place to Go*, Ken Worpole highlights that in the UK, two-thirds of 9–11-year-olds are dissatisfied with the quality of outdoor play facilities where they live. For 15–16-year-olds this rose to 81 per cent, higher than any other European country.[47] While there are numerous pockets of excellent spaces and creatively designed playgrounds used heavily by children, it needs to be recognised that children's lived experience of their neighbourhood often falls far short of that of their counterparts around the world.

Additionally, children's experiences of the public realm are not equal across the UK. As in Fleetwood, children living in some of the most economically deprived areas are particularly vulnerable to a poverty of experience in the built environment. Hence they suffer from 'double deprivation': an unequal distribution of both private wealth and public outdoor resources. One recent study found that deprived areas tend to have a much worse public environment than more affluent neighbourhoods – with more litter, frequent fly-tipping problems and worse maintenance of green space.[48] Moreover, they are often more densely populated than average, with a heavier dependence on and use of what public space is available, making them more susceptible to environmental wear and tear.[49] These spaces can also be more dangerous. Research has shown that children in the 10 per cent most deprived wards in England are more than three times as likely to be pedestrian casualties compared with those in the least deprived 10 per cent.[50]

The retreat from public space

As children and their parents become disillusioned with the quality and safety of the public realm, they retreat from it. The overall trends in Britain point towards less outdoor play, an increasing reliance on private transport, increased parental anxiety and less freedom for children and young people.

In 1993, a comparative study of German and English school children's travel patterns found that nearly a third of English children in the survey were collected from school by car – almost four times the proportion of the same age group of German children.[51] More recently, Department of Health data indicated that the number of 5–10-year-olds who walk to school fell from 61 per cent in 1992/93 to 52 per cent in 2002/03.

Children play outside less than they want to, and the amount of time they spend outside is declining. A survey of 1000 children in Leicester found that '94 per cent of children wanted to spend more time out of the house'.[52] Research also found that 67 per cent of children aged between 8 and 10 and 24 per cent of 11–14-year-olds never go the park or shops alone.[53] In another survey, 44 per cent of parents reported that their children never or hardly ever play outside the home without adult supervision.[54]

A wealth of statistics indicate how closely the retreat from public space correlates with adults' fears for the safety of children. A Barnardo's study highlighted the result of such fears: 60 per cent of parents polled reported being very worried when their children were playing out. 'Stranger danger' was reported to be the biggest worry (66 per cent), followed by danger from traffic (60 per cent). Most respondents thought that their neighbourhood was unsafe for children, with 31 per cent rating it very unsafe and 39 per cent fairly unsafe.[55] Recently the Children's Society found that some 43 per cent of 1148 adults surveyed said that children should not be allowed out alone with friends until they were 14 years old.[56]

Not only do children go outside less, but once they are outside often they are not allowed to do what they'd like. In one national study 45 per cent of 500 children interviewed said that they were not allowed to play with water, 36 per cent were not allowed to climb trees, 27 per cent were not allowed to play on climbing equipment, and 23 per cent were not allowed to ride bikes or use skateboards.[57]

Consequences for children

In spring 2007 a Unicef report on children's wellbeing in developed countries provoked a national debate about whether the UK was failing its children. It made for stark reading. The UK ranked bottom of the table, below 21 other industrialised countries. Approximately 80 per cent of young people consider their health to be good or excellent in every OECD country except the UK. Over 20 per cent in the UK rate their wellbeing as only 'fair or poor', more than any other of the OECD countries.[58]

Although there are many reasons for physical and mental health problems, they are connected to the retreat from the public realm. In 2001, research published in the *British Medical Journal* concluded that the main solution to the growing childhood obesity epidemic was to 'turn off the TV and promote playing. . . . Opportunities for spontaneous play may be the only requirement that young children need to increase their physical activity.'[59]

The 'obesity crisis' is now one of the most publicised threats to the nation's health. The statistics on young people and obesity are especially startling: 20 per cent of 4-year-olds are overweight, while 8.5 per cent of 6-year-olds and 15 per cent of 15-year-olds are obese.[60] The government suggests that schools should timetable at least two hours per week to be spent on physical activity. However, this in itself is not enough to meet the total recommended levels of 30–60 minutes of activity per day – how they spend the rest of their time matters just as much. Moreover, the evidence indicates that adult patterns of exercise are set early on in life, meaning that the statistics on children's health are a particular cause for concern when it comes to the future of the nation's health. The direct financial cost of inactivity to the NHS is around £1 billion annually, with an additional cost to the economy estimated at around £2.3 to £2.6 billion; with current trends such figures are likely to rise further.[61]

In extreme cases what is known as 'play deprivation' may occur. This was described by Bob Hughes in 2003 as the result of 'a chronic lack of sensory interaction with the world: a form of sensory deprivation.'[62] A lack of interaction with the wider world has profound implications for mental health, particularly for the most vulnerable children. Early studies in this area found that irrespective of demography, a child deprived of play experiences is more likely to become highly violent and anti-social.[63]

Many of the responses to ill-health of young people and children have tended to focus either on the elimination of 'bads', such as limiting advertising to children and restricting the sales of fatty foods. Alternatively they focus on dealing with the surface symptoms of the problem. There have, for example, been many schemes to increase the number of children walking to school. But these can place excessive emphasis on changing the behaviour of young people when it might be as important to recognise the limitations placed on them by their immediate environment. For example, 'walking bus' schemes will collect groups of children to walk to school together and with adult guidance, but such schemes are unlikely to address the reasons why children would have stopped walking alone in the first place.

Public worries

Britain's anti-social behaviour anxiety is one clear symptom of the dysfunctional relationship between young people and public space. Although orders can be made against any person who has acted in an anti-social manner, nearly half have been made against people under 18.[64]

This forms part of a wider trend whereby many of the activities of young people are deemed to be deviant or even criminal. In local satisfaction surveys, taking action on young people now regularly tops the poll in terms of what people think will most improve their area, ahead even of health and education.[65] In a MORI survey 45 per cent of respondents thought anti-social behaviour orders (Asbos) were a good way of dealing with teenagers who are responsible for anti-social behaviour.[66]

David Lloyd George once said that 'the right to play is a child's first claim on the community. Play is nature's training for life. No community can infringe on that right without doing deep and enduring harm to the minds and bodies of its citizens.'[67] As the evidence stacks up that the UK is failing to uphold this right and the impacts are felt on children and communities, there is an urgent need to understand the systematic, cultural and institutional factors which have led to this situation. Only then can a different way forward be mapped out. The second part of this pamphlet picks up this challenge.

Part Two
Spaces, stories and shaping places

The first part of this pamphlet set out what can be gained from a healthy public realm for children and how what is currently on offer falls far short of that promise. Part Two seeks to understand why such a dysfunctional relationship between children and places has developed. Three issues are important:

Pressures on our built environment

Densification, the continued dominance of cars and assumptions about the functions of places determine the look and feel of the built environment. This chapter will argue that these pressures have an often overlooked negative impact on children and young people.

Attitudes towards children

Too often public discourses about children focus exclusively on them, rather than acknowledging the central role adult attitudes play. This chapter investigates the tension between the fear *for* children and the fear *of* children and young people, arguing that both narratives limit children's access to and use of the public realm.

Professional practices

Before change can happen in the way the public realm is designed, delivered and managed, we need to understand the barriers from the perspective of the wide number of professions involved in making places. The difficulties of collaboration and engaging with children meaningfully, coupled with the pressures specific to particular professionals, mean that creative, playful place-making is still a profound challenge for many.

03. Pressures on our built environment

The redevelopment of the Upper Horfield estate, to the north of Bristol, can be considered a success. Concrete cancer was discovered in the housing stock there in the late 1980s, forcing the council to redevelop the entire 600-house estate. Facing tight financial constraints and an increasingly sceptical community, the council formulated a novel housing association scheme aimed at overcoming the chronic lack of external public funding. The land was handed over to the newly formed Bristol Community Housing Foundation (BCHF). BCHF sold half the land to a private developer and used the proceeds to pay for the renewal of social housing while allowing the developer to build housing for the private sales market.

The result is a new community of 900 new-build units (over 1000 when completed), around half of which are private and half social rented. Its innovative genesis and management secured the scheme top prize at the *Guardian* Public Services Awards in December 2006.

But it is telling that even here, at this point of triumph, the story for children and young people is less uplifting. Although there is a creative street design that aims to favour children's freedom to play on the street, the children aren't able to use the space in the way they want to. As one of them, Tim, put it: 'One of us could be the next England player but we won't know because we can't practice. There's nowhere to play football.'

Two announcements on the noticeboard of the BCHF office communicates the predicament of the lives of young people in the neighbourhood: one announces evening activities organised by the BCHF; the other is a police dispersal order.

The built environment and young people

The experiences in Bristol chime with the broader story of urban regeneration.

In 2003, Stuart Lipton, former chairman of CABE, argued that 'we are the fourth wealthiest nation in the world, and yet we have chosen for a long time to dress ourselves in rags. As a society we seem now to accept the poverty of our streets and spaces.'[68] That has not gone unnoticed. Indeed, as Steven Johnson observes: 'There are few ideas more widely received these days than the premise that traditional urban environments – the kind with bustling footpaths, public squares, distinctive local flavour, elaborate street culture, and a diverse intermingling of people – have become an endangered species.'[69] In response to such a discourse of loss, the importance of improving public space has caught policy-makers' attention. Urban regeneration is high on the agenda across many parts of the country including housing estates, in town centres, in parks. Often, it is matched by significant investment – from both the public and private sector.

But the question remains whether this increased investment in places is benefiting children. Across the six case studies undertaken by Demos and Fundamental Architectural Inclusion as part of this research there was this powerful common story: the renewed focus on place-making and regeneration does not necessarily benefit children and young people. As one participant in the Demos place-shapers forum told us, 'children's problems are subsumed by the bigger public realm challenge'.

This chapter will talk of the consequences of that bigger public realm challenge and how it relates to young people. The case studies suggest three main issues that negatively affect children:

- The *quantity* of public space that children can readily access is diminishing.

- The *quality* of public space design, delivery and management restricts children's freedom and use of space.
- The current dominance of a user *hierarchy* – either explicit or implicit – in spaces and places marginalises children vis-à-vis other uses and users.

No space to go

With the UK embarking on a massive national housebuilding programme, the dynamics and pressures on social relations in the estate of Upper Horfield are revealing. As a high-density, low-rise, mixed-income housing estate, the estate is representative of many of the UK's new residential neighbourhoods. How children fare here has resonance and learning possibilities for other new communities like it.

A community development worker for the Upper Horfield Community Trust, a local residents' association, begins to explain the problem: 'The density of the new estate was a key concern from the start. There used to be a little green space called "the tip"; it was used by the primary school . . . that land was lost . . . now there is just concrete, for the schoolyard, and in the neighbourhood.'[70]

At the centre of the story of Upper Horfield are the difficulties the council had in finding money to fund the regeneration. To make the project viable, density had to increase by a factor of 1.5 and there was no room to negotiate. Oona Goldsworthy, BCHF chief executive, explains: 'The margins were really tight. We'd had years of failing to make the project happen. In the end, we had to just get this built.'[71] Although there were different design options, this density was a given.

Coincident with these economic and planning pressures was an approach to the layout based on Home Zone principles,[72] designed to make the streets themselves playable, instead of

creating separate playgrounds. However, while the physical design permitted play, the cultural and social attitudes of adult residents in practice prevented the streets being used for play. As such, the effective amount of playable space in the estate has declined dramatically.

The density of new-build residential developments is on the rise across the UK not just because of cost considerations. It has become a hallmark of the urban renaissance agenda and new housebuilding drive as presented in the Sustainable Communities plan.[73] Densities for new residential developments have increased from 25 dwellings per hectare in 1997 to 40 dwellings per hectare in 2005.[74]

The density agenda has an environmental rationale: building in higher densities preserves open land and enables increased provision of local services and public transport, hence reducing the need to use a car. Higher densities are also highly profitable for housebuilders. The Land Registry figures from April 2007 show that house prices rose 9.1 per cent between 2006 and 2007,[75] continuing a long-term upward trend. One survey found that the price of land rose by around 800 per cent in the 20 years to 2003.[76] It is in this climate that developers have been keen to jump on the density bandwagon en masse.

Density in itself is not the problem; high-density housing can contain excellent places for children. However, all too often it leads directly to loss of green space. The National Playing Fields Association found in 2005 that as many as four out of ten school and community playing fields in England have been lost since 1992[77] – sold off to make way for housing to pay for school rebuilding or other urban development.

This loss of playable space is particularly problematic in areas with a relatively high number of children. June Barnes, chief executive of East Thames Group Housing Association, sees the same problem: 'Hyper-dense housing is an issue. Too often these places are internally overcrowded, are built without balconies, and open spaces are limited in such projects – plus, the open spaces that are there, are often exclusive.'[78] She emphasises therefore that, contrary to the current trend for denser and denser projects, a greater diversity of types of new development should be encouraged, including building in lower densities. For the same reason, a study by the London chapter of the National Housing Federation recommends working towards 'maximum child densities' per estate to ensure residents' quality of life.[79]

The quality deficit

Developers will make big profits on anything with four walls and a roof at the moment, because of the state of the UK housing market.

Participant, Demos place-shapers forum

Making space for children is not just an issue of quantifying available space; young people's problems are equally linked to the *quality* of spaces. As one study put it, 'the worse a local environment looks, the less able children are to play freely'.[80] Theoretically accessible space becomes unusable if it is unattractive or feels unsafe. In that context, green space managers are being forced into trade-offs between quantity and quality. For example in Bolton one green space manager advocated the selling off of open space, and even playgrounds: 'There are many without any play value. They are in the wrong place, badly maintained, dangerous. If we sold them off and got the money, we could actually increase the quality of places for young ones here.'[81] Experience elsewhere, however, reveals how difficult it is to ring-fence money from selling off green space for public realm improvements, with monies tending to be recycled into general local authority spending.

The funding issue

In the early 1990s, Heywood Park in Bolton was a flagship play environment. With the needs of disabled children in mind, a sensory garden was created in one part of the park: a groundbreaking example of an inclusive play garden, with full disabled access and innovative play equipment. Despite its relatively small size and location in an otherwise unremarkable Bolton neighbourhood, with low-rise houses mixed with old cotton mills and newer industrial estates, families would come to Heywood Park from miles away and from surrounding towns.

After the first few years, however, the park went into decline. Fifteen years later, only the sturdy German-made responsive soundscape remains of the original garden. The flowerbeds are empty and there are signs of recent fires. With its deserted paths, the former play garden has the feel of a disused, unwelcoming space. A new playground has been built next to it, attached to a council-run play centre – but, as detailed below, this too is experiencing problems.

Much of this is down to the lack of ongoing funding for maintenance, as the manager responsible for Heywood Park said: 'Lots of it comes down to money. We still face year on year cuts.'[82] That story resonates across Britain. Despite their importance to the quality of life and vitality of our communities, the last decades have seen dramatic cuts in expenditure on parks and public spaces, which are now estimated to be in the region, cumulatively, of £1.3 billion.[83] Investment in urban parks and open spaces dropped from 44 per cent of local authority spending in 1976/77 to 31 per cent by 1998/99. An audit by the Policy Studies Institute revealed that fewer than one in five of all parks is in good condition.[84] Only recently has the nationwide decline in funding begun to be reversed, but it is acknowledged that this reversal is not yet sufficient to make up for the structural and accumulated neglect of the past.[85]

Play space as afterthought

But the quality problem is not just the result of lack of maintenance. An additional problem is the poor quality of much new urban development. An example from new housebuilding makes this clear: in 2006 the Commission for Architecture and the Built Environment (CABE) published evaluations of new housing schemes across the country. The research found that only 18 per cent of newbuild earned a design rating of good or very good, with the vast majority being assessed as 'average' (ie mediocre – 53 per cent) or, in the case of 29 per cent, so poor that they should never have been given planning permission.[86] In particular the research found that 'schemes frequently had a poorly structured layout, leading to a poor quality streetscape, a lack of distinction between public and private realms, and a development that was difficult to navigate, with . . . dominant roads and poorly integrated car parking', and 'public open space was often poorly designed or maintained'.

Within such low-quality developments, play space is one of the first elements to suffer. Playgrounds, for example, are an afterthought in the urban development process, included only to satisfy planning conditions. As one local authority officer revealed:

When developers build out a scheme, they have to stick their equipment shed somewhere, usually close to the main road for access. When they are all done, that bit of leftover land becomes the playground – often in the worst possible position. That's why we are not enthusiastic about developers doing their own playgrounds on site – because they are useless.[87]

Boredom rules

There is a more general problem with playgrounds: they are often not what children want. In the case studies children spoke about wanting to play football, and to play outside. Rarely did they speak about wanting more playgrounds as such. Yet as the rest of the public realm has declined over several decades there has been an increasing emphasis on such enclaves of play provision. With tiny budgets for maintenance, the most straightforward easily serviced play equipment often seems preferable. Equally, heavy pressure to minimise risks and liability in the public realm contributes to a sense of there being a series of standardised play areas: safety surfacing and metal frame equipment has become the standard. As CABE found in its study 'Living with risk: promoting better public space design', pressures to minimise liability in the public realm have created a culture of 'playing it safe' with standardised spaces lacking in creativity.[88] These safety-first spaces offer little excitement and challenge of the kind that children need.

This might not be too disconcerting if the only outcome for children was boredom. However, play facilities often offer so little stimulation that children may be tempted to go elsewhere, to places that are more dangerous for them.

Fragmentation or integration?

Tyler Above a certain age, I'd say above like 11, 12, you don't want play facilities, you want literally open space and some seats.

Jamie Yeah, no one in our school would think 'play a game' you just want to sit down.

The standard playground offer also gives little to older children. Even though in principle, it is possible – and often necessary – to design specific play spaces for different age groups, the trend towards designated, targeted playgrounds for a narrow age range is problematic. As Peter Lipman, from the sustainable transport charity Sustrans, says: 'The focus on playgrounds is an admission of defeat – you have to look at the entire streetscape, the sort of spaces that everyone uses.'[89] Tim Gill, former director of the Children's Play Council, calls this 'playable space' – space that facilitates play, rather than prescribing any particular use, as a springy chicken does.

This is the central challenge of children and the public realm: to what extent is the public realm as a whole playable? The reality across the case studies for this research showed that space is fragmented and segregated, with small spaces that are suitable for children but large areas in between where they cannot go. For example, Heywood Park sits in a chaotic network of poorly maintained public spaces. The roads that surround the park on three sides effectively form a border, dominating the local space. Across from the park sits a housing estate, at the corner of which lies a small playground, nestled in a patch of land beside the road. It sits embarrassed in the shadow of the larger park, and represents the typical piece of playground without any actual play value. A few metres away there is a school, with high walls demarcating its boundaries.

Even the park itself is highly segregated. A bowling green caters to the elderly but excludes the young; a newly built all-weather football pitch is dominated by older teenagers. The new children's playground and play centre dominates the middle of the park, bearing little relation to the former sensory garden described above. Nevertheless, interviews with young people in the park found that for younger children the park provides a welcoming and engaging play space, and the play area is well looked after. Although the aesthetics of the park – its abandoned corners and the failed play garden – might suggest a less than ideal space, the park still provides a place that answers many of the needs of younger children.

Meanwhile, young people are less frequent users of the park, and were nostalgic for a time when they had enjoyed coming to the park, a time when they had felt the park was still theirs. They felt they had lost ownership over the place, and that they needed traditional 'youth' facilities in the park such as a shelter, both for practical reasons (somewhere to spend time that was dry and comfortable) and for symbolic reasons (to give them a legitimacy to be in the park). The main problem they identify is fear. At night the park is unsafe because of fights, drugs and drinking. This view is echoed by the youth workers who complain about the lack of provision in the area. While the council play centre is very well funded for the younger children, there is hardly any money for the youth work in the same area, contributing to the 'nothing to do, nowhere to go' situation so typical of youth experience of places across Britain.

This park can be seen as a microcosm of a problem visible across the broader public realm: segregated space is matched by segregated ages and segregated services. The council's play service, the youth service, the park's maintenance service and the road maintenance contractors all take care of some part of the public realm and its activities, but together this does not constitute a positive play offer to children and young people, or indeed to adults.

The area around Heywood Park is also falling short of young people's needs. Some of the young people report that they avoid the park and other public spaces in the neighbourhoods altogether, retreating into their homes or friends' places. It was striking that, for such a large area, the alternatives to hanging around Heywood were limited if not non-existent, making the dominance of the park by 'problem' youngsters particularly significant and damaging. The streetscape of much of the surrounding area is in strikingly bad shape. Large amounts of derelict space were visible alongside small playgrounds or patches of grass. The roads punctuate these spaces formidably. As a result, what could be one coherent green space and young person's domain, between school and housing estate and park, is in fact a set of unconnected patches of land, some in a good state, some utterly unwelcoming.

At the bottom of the hierarchy

There is a third issue that cuts across both the quantity and quality of public spaces: the question of what they are actually *for*. Despite the very real problems of funding and development pressure in Bristol and Bolton we found that children (outside the places designed especially for them) are at the bottom of a user hierarchy of public space that seems to be unconsciously assumed across Britain. Over the past decades, two other uses of the public realm have been consistently privileged above play: cars and commerce.

The continued dominance of cars

There is no doubt that the greatest single factor affecting children's personal autonomy in the twentieth century. . . has been the loss of the street. . . to the car.

'Play, participation and potential'[90]

They should ask us what should happen to this place. Because if it was an adults' park it would be a car park; they love car parks.

Katie, Bristol

Katie is articulating what we all know: adults love cars and having places to put them. Cars are more visible in the public realm than children – there are now around 33 million cars in Britain[91] compared with around 11 million dependent children.[92]

Both children and adults considered traffic to be one of the main factors that stop children and young people playing or spending time in the streets or areas near their homes, with nearly one in four children and one in three adults listing it as one of their top three barriers to street play.[93] Across all the case studies children and young people voiced their resentment at the dominance of cars.

In Upper Horfield's attempts to counter the dominance of the car were designed in to the redevelopment. As we saw, in order to make up for a lack of play space, a core ambition was to improve the space between houses – *streets*. Upper Horfield has been designed as a Home Zone,[94] a novel approach to street layout design that encourages cars and pedestrians to share the same surface, obliging cars to give priority to children. Whereas it does not solve all problems (as one playworker put it, 'shared space does not work if it just means more kids on less space'[95]), it is one of the more successful aspects of the estate. The Upper Horfield Community Trust worker says that there are visibly more children playing on the street in the new estate than in the surrounding areas.[96]

Home Zones point to a potential change in how streets can be used in the UK – and it is one that observers think could become increasingly relevant in the future. But a mother of one of the children in Bristol was more sceptical: 'Upper Horfield is now a little pedestrian-friendly island, but it is still surrounded by big roads – and I still worry when my children go out.'[97]

There is no doubt that children sometimes benefit from the car: structural changes in the spatial make-up of our towns, cities and neighbourhoods and the nature of leisure and service provision have led to greatly increased distances between vital services. To get to places, families often struggle without private transport. However, as Mayer Hillman argues recently, the lure of far-away attractions and the resultant depopulation of local neighbourhoods and streets can have a negative impact on children:

The local environment now has fewer attractions and its amenity has been lowered: vehicle fumes increasingly pollute the air and traffic noise makes conversation difficult. Children, much more reliant on getting about on foot or. . . on a bicycle, are exposed to more danger.[98]

In this context, streets serve primarily as routes for transportation rather than sites of social interaction. The experiences of those in Upper Horfield suggest that formal changes to streets, emphasising shared usage, will not alone interrupt the dominance of the car. There is the further problem of this narrower conception of streets. Even where good-quality public space or parks do exist, children are often forbidden from walking to them because of parental fears of busy roads. For this reason, the focus needs to be on networks of streets and the overall ecology of spaces and places and how they connect.

But the dominance of the car is not the only use of the public realm that is sidelining children. Although they are the primary factor in residential streets, children and young people also lose out against the imperatives of commerce. This is particularly visible in town centres. Here, Britain's regeneration effort is failing to create spaces where children and young people are part of the story.

Sidelining the young

The centres of Sheffield and Maidstone are environments that have difficulty accommodating young people. These are town centres in which all sides agree that young people are doing little *wrong*. But such is the nature of the space that there is largely nothing for them to do there beyond shopping. Compounding the problem is the fact that where there are places to spend non-shopping time young people are often not welcome in them.

The desire and the need to court private investment as the springboard for regeneration coincides with density pressures, negative perceptions of young people, and the trend towards privatising space. The result is a severe social blind-spot. The problem at the heart of this is what different spaces allow – or encourage – the public to do. The investment that has gone into the recent wave of regeneration, as part of the urban renaissance agenda, means that the principles on which places are created and managed are often driven by narrow economic interests. Even Lord Richard Rogers, who led the original Urban Task Force, acknowledges the problem, suggesting that the funding streams for regional development agencies have 'led them to focus on economic development, jobs and growth rather than high quality, well-designed, sustainable urban development'.[99]

To 'live, work and play' is the new mantra of mixed-use town centres. But 'play' in too many of these places means adults' play – monied play. For example, Planning Policy Statement 6 – the planning policy document guiding town centre development and regeneration – encourages the retail and nighttime functions of town centres, but does not acknowledge their role for children and young people.[100] Yet, as research by Helen Woolley and Ralph Johns has shown, young people 'are often drawn to the city centre by factors other than consumption, such as social interaction and… the green and open spaces in the urban fabric'.[101] A reductionist vision of town centres that sees them as simply conduits for consumption therefore fails children and young people.

Such economically driven public spaces are more supervised, managed and controlled than ever before. The architect Inderpaul Johar argues that no matter how these new developments are made to look, they are often not fully part of the public realm any more:

These spaces are 'designed' to attract and repel certain audiences through the projection of particular worldviews, be they explicit or more subliminal. . . They are highly serviced, programmed, mediated environments that look and behave like consumer products... For those gifted with sufficient resources for choice and mobility, these environs create popular, liberating, niche spaces... For the remaining minority of people, who are to various degrees immobile or disadvantaged, these spaces can trigger alienation [and] disempowerment.[102]

This disempowerment is clear in the increasingly narrow definition of acceptable public behaviour; as the function of spaces becomes more narrowly circumscribed, and more clearly targeted, so do expectations of what activities can happen in them. Many public places are subject to limits on noise, skateboarding, loitering, drinking and now smoking. Many of these restrictions are for valid reasons but, arguably, they also have the unintended consequence of edging out the 'playful' or the unexpected from our cities. And such conceptions of desirable and undesirable behaviour help to explain why children and young people – the least monied, those with the greatest tendency to simply 'hang about' – have been called the 'unacknowledged outsiders'[103] in the planning and management of our places, and have effectively been written out of the urban renaissance script.

04. Our stories about children

Design is important, but we have to accept it only has a limited role here – there are much wider issues that limit children.

Lamine Mahdjoubi[104]

Leah   I don't like when they put 'no balls' [notices].

Interviewer   How does that make you feel?

Leah   Sad cos you can't hardly play.

Interviewer   Who do you think puts up the notices?

Leah   The council because of old people.

Places are not just physically but also socially constituted. Children's and young people's position in public space is shaped not just by poor physical design, but also by cultural and media perceptions of youth and childhood in general. These perceptions create a powerful narrative which dictates children's negative experiences of the public realm.

The state of modern childhood sits prominently in the public consciousness and across the national media. In government, major strands of policy focus on young people, child poverty and education. There is no easy story of children being ignored, in policy or otherwise. But that does not mean that all the concern currently being generated around the issue of childhood is helpful.

Although children now constitute an entirely different social category, this was not always the case. Childhood is a relatively recent invention. In the Middle Ages children in Western Europe were regarded as mini-adults – only different in strength and mental abilities.[105] The idea of the universal childhood then emerged in the Renaissance and was given additional importance during the Romantic movement in the eighteenth century. In recent years this has lost credibility and instead childhood is understood in terms of the idea of 'many childhoods' shaped, for example, by mobility, ethnicity and poverty.[106] Yet there is still a tendency to present two polarised visions of children and childhood, and these play out directly into public attitudes to the presence of children in the public realm.

On the one hand society is becoming increasingly afraid *of* children, and on the other increasingly fearful *for* them. Young people are either 'victims of the city'[107] or they are perpetrators of violence and disturbers of the peace. The result is an inconsistent and unhelpful dichotomy between young people who need to be protected from the dangers of the outside world, and those we want to be protected from. Both narratives are based on a fearful relationship to the public realm.

This chapter explores the role of attitudes towards young people in shaping the public realm. Beyond verbal acknowledgement that 'not all teenagers are the same', the case studies showed that there is too little effort to understand how adult attitudes shape young people's behaviour and in turn contribute to the overall quality of the public realm for everyone.

Intolerance of children

Adults don't seem to want shared space. They don't go to places that could be shared space – we need to raise the awareness of the effects that adults have on children.

Play and youth officer, Bristol[108]

Every morning I have 20 messages on my phone from residents complaining about kids playing with a ball on some grass.

Open space manager, Fleetwood[109]

I am sick to death of being expected to 'suffer the children' in public places. I do not want children of my own so I certainly do not want my life constantly interrupted by whining, crying, badly behaved off-spring appallingly managed by incompetent and disinterested parents. There are suitable places to take children and there are very definitely places where children should not be allowed. Why should everyone else have to put up with families who clearly don't give a damn about how socially acceptable they are, who seem unaware that they spoil and ruin events and environments?

Contributor to BBC discussion radio show[110]

In Maidstone, there is a corner of the town centre where young people and older children congregate after school. It is the spot to get on and off the buses on their way home. The young people like to stand socialising in large groups with their friends. But the area is also a main route for shoppers and office workers.

A number of complaints were received about this daily routine; some people were uncomfortable walking past these young people. A long-term struggle ensued, with the aim of breaking-up the hanging around culture. This has so far met with no success; the space was part of those children's daily lives and the practice of meeting there proved too ingrained and resistant to change. Even when the police brought in sniffer dogs to intimidate them, the young people just petted the dogs and ignored the presence of the police. It seems that irrespective of whether children and young people as those in Maidstone are doing anything wrong, they are simply offending many people with their presence. In some town centres this struggle for territory can be repeated many times as young people are dispersed from one space, only to colonise another.

Whether the spaces are residential, commercial or public the same battles are being played out all over the UK. The quotations cited above, detailing the complaints green space managers received, are symptoms of the same problem. Professionals

managing public space find themselves having to respond to
these attitudes on a daily basis. In many ways adult intolerance
of children has been a constant of public life – in *The Child in
the City*, Colin Ward talks of the existence of 'land-use' conflict
between children and adults. Evidence he cites includes how:

in 1385 the Bishop of London complained of Ball Games around St
Paul's... while in the 19th century 'there were repeated complaints
that the pavements of London were made impassable by children's
shuttlecock and tipcat.'[111]

Even if there is nothing new about the phenomenon of
adult intolerance (and children's protest through play) there is
reason to be particularly concerned now. Chapter 2 explored how
young people's behaviour is beginning to be deemed criminal.
The British Crime Survey now categorises 'young people hanging
around' as one of seven questions about people's experience of
anti-social behaviour. In its 2006 findings, the BCS reports that
'the most widely perceived ASB (anti-social behaviour) problems
were young people hanging around and rubbish or litter; just
under a third of people regarded these a "very" or "fairly" big
problem'.[112] Below the headline figures, what is interesting is the
disparity between different people's view as to what constitutes
anti-social behaviour.

Evidence suggests that young people have a very nuanced
understanding of what anti-social behaviour means. A report
by YouthNet and the British Youth Council found that ASB is
defined by young people primarily as threatening, offensive,
damaging or violent behaviour – specifically, behaviour
that directly infringes on other people's rights or freedoms.
Hanging around with friends in public and wearing a hoodie
are considered anti-social by only 2 per cent and 6 per cent of
respondents, respectively.[113] Young people we spoke to in Sheffield
drew clear distinctions between how they behave when socialising
in groups, and more problematic behaviour of excessive drinking
and drug-taking. One girl said that city ambassadors – those

charged with managing the space – 'should keep an eye on young people and actually realise, before they move them on, *what they are actually doing*'.

But it is adults who set the bounds of social behaviour. Young people have little voice with which to complain that the way adults treat them is anti-social. The result is that *any* social behaviour of young people can be labelled as *anti*-social. The prevalence of anti-social behaviour is as much a symptom of this lack of tolerance and trust, as it is about poorly behaved youth.

During the research for the case studies the police described receiving complaints from adults about children who, although not doing anything illegal, were irritating or alarming them by gathering in groups. For example, a police officer in Fleetwood said:

It's an age old problem, kids want to find a place to hang out, adults don't want them to be there. I wish there was somewhere we could send them when we move them along... it isn't through badness, it's through boredom.[114]

This underlying tacit – or overt – disapproval from adults of the everyday presence of young people in public was backed up by the experience of park and play officers. One explained: 'Exclusion of children from shared space does not come from legislation like the ASBO regime but from adult behaviour and attitudes.'[115] Nevertheless, in the process of targeting genuinely unacceptable behaviour, the Respect Agenda and ASBOs may also inadvertently legitimise a lack of tolerance towards young people.

This intolerance manifests itself in the proliferation of 'no ball games' signs; playgrounds or youth shelters being built out of sight; and the issuing of dispersal orders. In Bristol, it went so far as one resident telling the Upper Horfield Community Trust worker that 'if they put in a new football pitch I will take it down with my own hands'.[116]

Bad behaviour, violence or deliberate intimidation is not something anyone should have to accept. However, the line between what constitutes behaviour that is unacceptable and the social behaviour of young people has become difficult to distinguish, and the intolerance of adults is now one of the most powerful factors that limits the freedom of children and young people in the public realm.

Play as transgressive behaviour

Children and young people are particularly vulnerable to the zeal for behaviour management that we discussed in the previous chapter. Early adolescence and childhood are periods for testing boundaries and, in conjunction with peers, developing a sense of self away from the family. As a result, young people's behaviour can be challenging to wider society. Playful behaviour is by no means frivolous in the development of children; at its essence it can be transgressive.

This is important when considering the recent responses to the perception of poorly behaved young people. There have been welcome moves that acknowledge the need to provide them with activities and places to go. But these tend not to make the connection between the poor relationship between young people and the spaces and people around them and the attitudes *towards* young people. The Respect Action Plan, for example, and its reference to the Youth Opportunity Fund, is framed around the idea of young people changing how they behave so they make a 'positive contribution'.[117] Most recently the UK government announced a ten-year strategy for positive activities for young people.[118] Launching that, Ed Balls, Secretary of State for Children, Schools and Families, said: 'It is about kids having interesting things to do and it is about young people having respect for the society in which they live.'[119] And the Communities and Local Government department makes a commitment to 'discover how we're making sure children and young people have their say and grow up to be responsible citizens'.[120]

These are certainly positive moves; structured activities for young people are undeniably important.[121] But there needs to be a recognition that *unstructured* activities in public space are part of what growing up is about. As one youth worker in Maidstone told us: 'There are now more activities for young people – a music festival, sports development – all that is positive in its own right. But the physical structure of the town does not work; it is car-dominated and hostile. They just need to be kids!'[122] Even if young people are offered more activities, the problem remains that young people are not welcome in public places unless they have been specifically designed for them.

Perceiving danger

Much of the more sensational coverage of young people has echoes of Lionel Trilling's observation that the 'great modern theme' is the 'child's elemental emotions and familial trusts being violated by the ideas and institutions of modern life'.[123] A sense of loss and fear pervades public discourses, with modern childhood now famously condemned as 'toxic'.[124] The role of parents, teachers and professionals in this narrative is to offer children protection from this harmful environment.

Four out of five adults believe that life for children in Britain is more dangerous than it used to be.[125] This is despite the risk of abduction or murder of children being stable, and the likelihood of children dying from injury falling steadily since the 1970s.[126]

A nostalgic golden era for children is mourned for. As Colin Ward observes, we use our view of the 'ideal childhood' to:

. . .reshape our own memories, we may try to recreate it for our children or we may judge *them* according to the degree to which they inhabit it too. . . It sifts through our selective and self-censored memory as a myth and idyll of the way things ought to be, the lost paradise to be regained.[127]

Given this sense of a 'lost paradise' and the rising anxiety about the wellbeing of children, the reluctance to let children roam beyond the confines of the family home or school is unsurprising. Thomas and Hocking explain this as a tendency to 'enclose childhood, corralling it into dedicated spaces and institutions, when, in fact, we need to learn how to integrate it into the whole of society, without losing, ignoring or destroying its unique features.'[128]

Many of the children in the case studies were aware that their worlds would be much smaller if they responded to all their parents' fears:

Interviewer   Would you say this place has any reputation?

Connor   Mmmmh yeah it does, amongst adults. My mum used to tell me not to come here because it was dodgy. Well, at night it is definitely something to avoid cos there's no lighting.

Interviewer   Do you feel safe here?

Connor   I do. I shouldn't given what's happened in the past.
          When I was 15 a friend got his braces kicked through his
          lips just down there and it didn't get caught on camera
          but I don't really feel scared. It's possible it could happen
          but it's a rare occurrence.

Interviewer   Do you tend to come here with mates?

Connor   Oh yeah definitely. I would never try and kill time on my
          own up here.

Interviewer   In your opinion if there were more staff working here
               would it be safer? More attractive to come to?

Connor   It would, but it would be less attractive to come to.

Nasser   Less people would come to the park. It would feel like
          somewhere at school basically, no freedom.

Comparatively speaking (even when measured against other
developed nations) British parents overestimate risks, reducing
young people's freedom of movement as a result. For example,
it is telling that the UK came bottom of the Unicef rankings for
child wellbeing, but was the second most successful country when
it came to preventing accidents.[129]

So what is childhood for . . . ?

Everybody's different and I think they should look more into that and
not just oh cos you're a teenager. . .

Lewis, Sheffield

Not all teenagers are like that, in fact it's not many that are like that.

Ryan, Sheffield

As we saw in the last chapter, understanding what comprises a healthy public realm is intimately bound up with visions of what a good city is. The process of creating spaces for children is equally bound up with notions of what childhood is for and what constitutes a good childhood. For example, Deacon Academy, a new £46.4 million city academy school designed by Norman Foster, came under fire this year for plans for it to be built without a play area. The outlook of headteacher Alan McMurdo is revealing: 'I think what the public want is maximum learning.'[130]

Although in the government's Every Child Matters programme 'enjoyment' and 'achievement' are identified as part of the same headline outcome for children, and despite the government's affirmation about the importance of play, in practice resources remain directed towards educational attainment and away from play for play's sake. Asked about the most significant change to provision for young people in the recent past, a youth worker in Sheffield reported: 'All services from the council now are measurable; they are about productive outputs centred on learning and employment. There's no attention to the emotional and personal needs that young people have.'[131]

The emphasis on appreciating young people and their need to play is not just a case of offering a hug and providing a nicer set of swings. It is about appreciating the diverse needs and behaviour of children and young people across the places they experience in their everyday lives – between the home, the school and the public realm. There is no doubt that children are being accorded new rights and are being introduced into decision-making processes in an unprecedented way. The recent past has seen not just the Every Child Matters agenda but also Youth Matters, a proliferation of youth parliaments and youth forums, and the Young Advisors scheme, which allows young people a voice at the table for decision-making that affects them – although those processes remain heavily structured by adults.

Most importantly, beyond these formal schemes, young people are not gaining voice and influence in a sustained, everyday and informal way. The duality in the dominant approach to children, which conceives adults as either young people's protectors or their adversaries, has created barriers when it comes to listening and responding to their views.

Attitudes and policies towards children tend to be framed around an instrumentalised view of childhood, with the focus on a child's preparedness to become an economically productive member of society. Such narratives and the beliefs that sustain them are not easy things to change, so for a culture shift to take place it is essential that we find out how they become institutionalised into professional and organisational practice.

05. Shaping places
for wellbeing

Interviewer   What do you think has made you feel that this is your space?

Mia   I don't know. It just feels like a place for young people to go. It's just. . . it looks fun. The water makes it even better. You can listen to it and relax, watch it.

The new Peace Gardens in the centre of Sheffield are a powerful symbol of the past decade of regeneration in the city. Sitting in the centre beside the town hall, its cascading water fountains, green spaces and banked sides attract lunch-time workers, respite-seeking shoppers, elderly people and the young alike. The heavy emphasis on investment in physical regeneration – a concerted effort to improve the public sphere – was a key part of the city's postindustrial transition. There is now to be a strong network of pedestrianised routes linking the city centre to Sheffield's railway station. The Peace Gardens, like so much of the redevelopment of the city, seem to embody good design principles, high investment and joined-up working.

But like the other case study areas, Sheffield is no straightforward story of success or failure. Children and young people described feeling unwelcome when in groups and a general lack of understanding of how or why they want to use the space. Hence, the creation of a beautiful physical public space is let down by the way that the space is *socially* reproduced on an everyday basis.

This example makes clear that a good place offered to children and young people, unlike a playground or a youth club building, cannot just be *delivered*. Like many prized social goods – health, education, belonging – its realisation is more complex, depending on the active participation and 'co-production' of different players, for example between teachers, pupils and parents in the case of education. When it comes to producing healthy public spaces the relationships are equally complex.

The Sheffield story is in many ways typical of our case study areas in terms of getting part of the story right – in this case, the physical design. In Bolton, good children's play provision within the park was let down by scant youth provision, and a hostile wider public realm. In Maidstone, the promise of a youth café and increased activities for young people do not make up for the fact that they have little to do in the town centre overall. In Bristol, the innovative Home Zone concept does not compensate for the quantitative lack of play space, nor has adults' behaviour when driving changed sufficiently to give meaning to the underlying concept of 'shared space'. In Fleetwood, the community pressure to create a good local space for children and young people is struggling to compensate for the lack of resources and quality spaces.

To understand why so many good initiatives do not add up, it is essential to grasp more fully how the places that make up the public realm are being shaped. Just as Demos grounded the case studies in the everyday experiences of children and young people, so we also mapped the experiences of the people who created these spaces locally. We called these people 'place-shapers' – the people who plan our towns, manage our city centres or parks or design our roads. The way they work individually and together helps determine the way places look and feel – both for young people and adults. In-depth

The Lyons Inquiry into Local Government set out a role for local government as the voice of a whole community and an agent of 'place'. This role includes building and shaping local identity, and making sure that the right services are provided to local people based on local needs and preferences.[132]

The recent planning white paper, *Planning for a Sustainable Future*, signals a new commitment from government to improve the way the planning system works and positions planning as central to the place-shaping role of local authorities.[133]

For the purpose of this research we used a wider interpretation of this definition and took it to include all those local actors whose agency conditions the local built environment physically as well as socially – through commissioning, designing, delivering and maintaining public spaces such as squares, streets, playgrounds and parks, but also through their actions as surveillance personnel, in youth services, through to local advocacy organisations.

The aim was to understand the importance of factors both within and *outside* what can roughly be called 'the play sector', uncovering the diversity of professional practices that influence children

and young people's experiences. As such, across the six case studies we spoke to:

- community volunteers
- housing association managers
- housing developers
- landscape architects
- local authority green space managers, parks and play officers
- local authority parks maintenance managers
- local authority planning officers
- local authority traffic engineers
- local council members
- local police officers
- play service workers
- regeneration managers
- residents and the elderly
- town centre managers
- youth workers.

The conversations were held as semi-structured interviews, focusing on:

- the individual's interpretation of his/her job (or role) and their responsibilities and objectives
- the factors influencing the individual's view of children and young people in public space
- their contacts with other place-shaping agents in addressing issues about children and young people in the public realm
- the skills required to deal with young people
- incentives for and barriers to change in current practice.

interviews with a cross-section of place-shapers were undertaken in each of the six case study areas.

Three themes emerged from the research and conversations with the place-shapers across the six case study areas:

- Many place-shaping professionals have difficulties seeing and understanding how their work relates to the needs of children and young people.
- Many place-shaping professionals lack the capacity, skills and resources to engage with children effectively.
- Many find collaboration with other place-shaping professionals across the public, voluntary and community sectors difficult but essential to bring about change.

After exploring these three issues, the rest of this chapter will go on to map some of the successful tactics and approaches that were being used to negotiate new ways of working to provide better outcomes for children.

The invisibility of children and young people

For planning, highways and housing it can come as a surprise that the needs of young people are under their remit.

Public space coordinator, EC1 New Deal, London[134]

Responsibility for how a place works stretches across a large number of professionals, from the development negotiations of the planning department to the informal policing decisions of community support teams. Their sense of professionalism 'structures the exercise of power in everyday life'[135] – through their position they direct resources and effort, as well as setting the tone for public behaviour.

However, many place-shaping professionals are insufficiently aware of the role that they play in children's lives. Place-makers can inadvertently privilege other duties or other users of space. As one of the attendees at the Demos place-shapers forum said, 'While no one will disagree that play is important, very few see it as their priority or even co-responsibility.'

For example, one town centre manager, when asked what he saw as his primary job responsibility, responded without hesitation: 'Our job is to improve footfall in the town centre.'[136] Unsurprisingly, the quality of young people's experiences is thought to fall beyond the remit of most town centre management teams.

A similar scenario is evident for planners. Research from the field of urban studies raises concerns that children and young people have been 'conceptualised in urban planning as problem, and the result has been their marginalisation and increasing exclusion from a hostile urban environment'.[137] As already discussed, one policy document, PPS 6,[138] articulates a particularly childless view of town centres, and planners are bound by the policy on which they base decisions:

Within planning authorities, housing density can increase at the expense of public space. Huge swathes of free land are written off. Planners provide no indication of play. Within applications it is only bolted on at phase four as an afterthought, only in order to meet the tick box. . .

Participant, Demos place-shapers forum

In transport, the marginalisation of child-friendly policy and practice is also felt, as one transport planner confirmed at the Demos place-shapers forum:

At conferences, those of us interested in walking and cycling seem to still occupy the lunatic fringe. . . and until recently, even at the Department for Transport, walking and cycling was lumped together with 'local charging', ie the Congestion Charge – all the small, innovative do-good stuff.

Another transport planner described the difficulties within his local authority department:

There have been times where there was a real opportunity for doing better – shared spaces, cutting back on parking, putting in traffic calming... but through opposition within the Department we defaulted back to parking everywhere, and a bad layout... it's a real fight against routines.

Why children's voices aren't being heard . . .

We plan to give them [young people] more say in the way local services and activities are provided and to increase their choice... we will put spending power in the hands of young people, and give them influence to shape the activities available locally.

Youth Matters, Ruth Kelly's 'Foreword'[139]

Government has become ambitious in its plans for children and young people to be involved in decision-making that affects them to help create policy which reflects their needs and aspirations. But there is considerable divergence about how and when young people should be consulted. While there are debates about the effectiveness and indeed the legitimacy of such formal participation mechanisms such as youth councils,[140] there can be huge benefits in participative governance for everyone, including:

- Better, more responsive services
  Services are more tailored to the needs of individuals, and are quicker to respond to changes in those needs.

- Countering disengagement from politics and democracy
  Along with democratic renewal participation enhances trust in and positive engagement with services.

- Building social capital
  Enhances community cohesion, improves the quality of people's lives, and strengthens individual relationships.[141]

However, the case studies for this report revealed that on-the-ground, high-quality, timely and sustained engagement and consultation was often not taking place. This view is corroborated by a recent MORI poll for the Office of the Children's Commissioner, which found that half of young people feel they do not get enough say in decisions that affect them; only 18 per cent feel that they do.[142]

There are real political reasons behind this lack of meaningful engagement, as one participant in the Demos place-shapers forum outlined:

People who respond to the institutional structures are voters. Kids are therefore pushed to the wayside. Within this low-risk society the majority of decisions are dominated by those who shout very loudly or by those who focus on the negatives.

There is little political incentive to challenge the views of voting adults who vociferously complain about young people in their area. For example, one councillor in Fleetwood described the political risk he took in pushing through plans for a skateboard park: 'The number of complaints I had, I thought I might not get elected next time around.'[143]

These political disincentives are compounded by constraints on time and resources to embark on the kind of long-term engagement programmes that are likely to build better mutual understanding between young people, children and place professionals. In Bolton, the green space officer explained:

We haven't really got the engagement model right here. In other, smaller parks with a clear community voice it is much easier, but here we would really have to put in extra capacity – and it will be one, two years down the line before we will get there.[144]

Finally, skills and training to deal confidently and effectively with children and young people are lacking among many place

professionals. The case studies showed that there was a lack of 'engagement literacy'. This was cited as one of the main barriers to professionals speaking to children. Conscious that it demanded more time and expertise than engagement with adults, many simply avoided the issue. One youth worker already working towards putting better engagement into practice in Sheffield explained that:

The people doing the consultation often don't know how to respond to what young people are telling them. . . teaching professionals how to respond to young people's involvement is as important as the exhaustive consultation itself.[145]

However, better consultation is not just about listening and giving young people what they say they want. Professional expertise and mutual exchange of knowledge is also crucial. In consultation processes professionals play an important role in structuring the process and stimulating children to think beyond the only type of play provision they have encountered. The open space manager in Fleetwood experienced this directly:

When you first try and consult you find that all they wanted was a climbing frame and some springy chickens, they [parents and children] thought everything else looked unsafe.[146]

There are a number of benefits to enhancing levels of engagement literacy. Above all better communication between place professionals and children and young people offers a route out of the widespread and frustrating cycle of 'provide and destroy'.

I've seen play equipment brought in which lasts no more than a month before it gets trashed, because they had no idea what the children and young people actually wanted.

Housing association manager, Fleetwood[147]

Why collaboration holds the key

Bolton Homes [housing association] just see us as a provider of services. We don't *think* together.

Green space manager, Bolton[148]

Responsibility for the design, maintenance, planning and use of any space in the public realm is distributed across a vast number of departments, voluntary organisations and private companies. To make the space work for all users, including children, all of these stakeholders and agents need to be engaged in continuous partnership working linking the local and national levels.

Without a collaborative approach to place-making for young people change is hampered by fragmentation and a lack of shared language about the challenges let alone solutions. In the public realm, such problems have been compounded by drastic changes in public service delivery. The manager for Heywood Park complained that organisations with responsibility tended to see each other on a 'contractual basis', limiting the opportunities to collaborate away from the narrow remits of the organisation: 'They tend to see us as service providers.'[149] He and others pointed to the introduction of compulsory competitive tendering (CCT) as a key factor. Introduced in 1986, CCT requires local authorities to contract out the management and maintenance of public parks at the lowest price. This has played a part in allowing councils to reduce maintenance. But while efficiency might have been improved, there have been a number of detrimental consequences. The Bolton green space maintenance managers call it:

. . .a separation of responsibility and accountability – one contractor does the grass, the other the fences, the other the footpaths or the play equipment – but who does the *park*? That's why we are trying to take that all in-house again, to not just coordinate but also show the public: there is one person at the council responsible for this park.[150]

Across the case studies the needs of children and young people in public space fell in-between the cracks of professional responsibility. The difficulty of moving beyond this silo approach to collaborative practice is amply illustrated by the challenges of the new 'play strategy'.

Play strategies are local authority documents that outline a council's strategic approach to play provision. They provide a council with the space to speak of joined-up working and departmental responsibilities, and to begin to address some of the challenges of collaborative working. A survey of local authorities in England in 2001 found that 'less than 40 per cent had any kind of plan for play and that, on average, councils were spending less than 8p per child per week on outdoor play'.[151] Play strategies are a response to this lack of coherence in approaches to and resources behind play provision. As part of the Children's Play initiative, the money allocated by the Big Lottery Fund to local authorities to improve local provision for play is linked to the development of cross-cutting play strategies and implementation plans.

The *Planning for Play* guidance,[152] supporting the development of local play strategies, is clear that play strategies need to be about more than just play spaces, and should also look to build 'a more child-friendly public realm and greater recognition of the importance of play across the range of policy areas that have an influence on children's lives'. In many places they have highlighted the significance of play to a new audience:

There has been more done for play in the past 18 months than in the past 15 years.
Housing association employee, Fleetwood[153]

In other local authorities, however, it was proving more difficult to engage all the necessary parties. The difficulties experienced in these areas are indicative of the problem of professional collaboration more broadly:

The play strategy has raised our profile with planners and transport. On paper it looks great, but there isn't an action plan – and planners still often ignore play in negotiations.

A play and green space worker in Bristol[154]

Incentivising change

So if the day-to-day aims and objectives of so many place-shaping professionals are currently disconnected from better engagement and outcomes for children, how can the two become better aligned? What could professionals gain from such an alignment? How can play strategies become more than well-meaning paper aspirations?

Breaking beyond the disparate motivations, interests and professional cultures of the place-shaping professionals is challenging. However, play strategies and the emphasis on child and youth engagement will have practical impact on the ground only if they are developed in conjunction with a range of other – less formal – strategies that have clear incentives and pay-offs for all those involved. These incentives include a halt to the wastefulness of provide and destroy, less vandalism and threatening behaviour, increased satisfaction with spaces – even, perhaps, increased footfall.

The next part of this chapter explores some approaches that have enabled professionals to create successful spaces, practices or partnerships.

Design influences the way the public sector approaches space. We need to get families back into design. If you're a responsible designer you need to talk to your customer. Kids can design, build and maintain their space. We should take a hands-on approach, led by example, led by design.

Landscape architect, Parklife designer of Spa Fields[155]

Tucked away in a corner of Clerkenwell in London is a small strip of green space called Spa Fields. This park has had a number of incarnations, as a burial ground, a haven for drinkers and now finally as a landscaped green space for workers on their lunch hour, families and, most importantly, the young people who have always had a strong sense of ownership over the space. As the public space coordinator for EC1 New Deal described the space prior to its transformation: 'If you wanted to design a park to encourage anti-social behaviour you would have designed Spa Fields.'[156]

The challenge of overhauling this space was taken on by Parklife with funding from EC1 New Deal, plus match funding found by Islington Greenspace. This project represented a tremendous challenge of partnership working on numerous levels. The project manager for Islington Council described the key elements behind the process as it had developed in Spa Fields:

The most important thing is to write the brief and get a team together to create a space: architects, planners, transport planners, quantity surveyors, youth providers. What's challenging is to map out a project thoroughly, to really reflect who needs to be on board, to really think how to push risk – the danger is to start too quickly.[157]

The location of Spa Fields and the diversity of its users made it a difficult space to design for. The area has been described 'as a kind of socio-economic, historical and spatial fault line, a place of great tensions and inexorable drifts'.[158] Many disaffected young people tended to congregate there from the estates surrounding the park. New creative industries had moved in meaning young professionals sought out the space at other times. Designing the park to meet such complex patterns of usage was the first hurdle. It was one of the unique factors of the project that rather than 'designing out' problem users there was to be a space specifically for them. The public space coordinator told us that:

This project would only work if the 'anti-social' children were on board . . . the brief from the outset was that it needed to be inclusive.[159]

In Spa Fields the process of working with young people to produce two shelters customised with graffiti was time-consuming and effort-intensive. Given the history of anti-social behaviour in the area, the buy-in of detached youth workers and of the police was essential. Everyone now recognises the significance of this piece of 'territory':

They have their space now, recognised by us, by the police, by Greenspace managers. We have helped them to create options that are good and that are theirs.
Safer Neighbourhoods team officer, Islington[160]

Across the case studies there were many instances of good practice. There was a series of 'ingredients' of success, but often they remained patchy or isolated. In Spa Fields, they came together most coherently. In places such as this professionals had forged new ways of overcoming the barriers to collaboration whether professional, institutional or attitudinal.

Co-producing space

Above all, Spa Fields reaffirms the power of imaginative design as process, not just outcome, linked to an open and inclusive notion of what a space is for. Parklife spent considerable time mapping the patterns of usage and spatial behaviour, reflecting on the needs and desires of different users. Time and again, professionals interviewed as part of the case studies made the case for more in-depth, design-oriented briefs for public space projects.

This can happen in different ways; in Fleetwood, the production of a play

space was initiated by children themselves. The children in the neighbourhood group 'Community Change' submitted their own model of the way they wanted the proposed sports and play facility to look on a disused piece of green land on the estate – the scheme has just received planning approval.

One boy who lives locally hit on one of the most obvious benefits of co-production:

Interviewer   What if you were involved in maybe designing it and partly building it. Would you take more care of it?

Steve   We'd make sure people don't graffiti on it. We'd make sure no one comes on it. . . bad boys or. . . No one would get on it while it's being built.

One of the important elements that distinguishes this approach from more superficial consultation is the extent to which children are empowered and seen as active contributors to their community. This points to an important finding from this case study, which should be of significance to wider society as well as professionals:

The big difference about this community is that where others have seen children as a problem they saw them as the solution.
Deputy head of local school, Fleetwood[161]

The power of the intermediary

Children and young people in Fleetwood have become part of the solution because of the continued efforts of several dynamic adults who have worked with them to build their confidence and capacity. Professionals can be wary of engaging directly with young people. Indeed, without the presence of a trusted intermediary they are perhaps right to proceed carefully. These intermediaries are essential in bridging the gap between young people and professionals; they act as cultural translators. They can be youth workers, teachers, volunteers, play workers or they could be a young person. They act as champions of children and young people and are an important point of reference for matching provision to need. For example, there are several young people's advocates in Fleetwood, including a housing association officer and the chair of West View Residents' Association, who took the young people directly to the council and helped them make their case directly for their community. As he puts it: 'You use what you've got don't you? And we've got lots of children here.'[162]

Towards empowered and collaborative professionals

'Different departments' and 'different responsibilities' are a poor excuse for not doing better. Wherever individuals within organisations – those who like play, those who make connections – have taken the initiative, outcomes are visible.

Greenspace projects and development manager, Islington[163]

One of the crucial steps in building a healthy public realm is creating a culture shift in the way in which the people on the frontline see their roles in relation to children and young people. When professionals have moved beyond their conventional roles children and young people are often the direct beneficiaries. For example, this was the case with the work of a local police officer from the Safer Neighbourhoods team in Spa Fields, Islington:

My main role is to keep people happy, reduce the fear of crime. I need to be responsive to local concerns, be guided by the community. . . but I can do that in ways that I find beneficial. Youth provision is on top of everyone's list, so we are active in that: creating programmes ourselves, or supporting others who want to. As a result, calls to the police drop dramatically – you can tell on a week-by-week basis.[164]

It is precisely this sort of willingness to move beyond prescribed roles which enables professionals to achieve results. Many institutions already recognise this role – the housing associations not just in Bristol and Fleetwood, but in many other places see children's activities as part and parcel of what they should be providing, despite often challenging resource constraints. This evidence of success could then be used to push through the next set of ambitious plans. The transformation of Spa Fields serves as an example of what is possible, as the Islington Greenspace projects and development manager explains:

At first I was literally forcing things through, but now I can show them that it works through example.[165]

The challenge for policy-makers is to find ways of scaling up this kind of practice and disseminating these ideas widely. The next chapter sets out a series of recommendations for embedding this kind of innovative thinking more widely across our public realm.

Part Three
Where next?

06. Conclusions and recommendations

In May 2006 London's traffic was suspended as the Sultan's Elephant trundled its way through the streets of the capital. The unfamiliar apparition gave the streets back to the people and delighted not just the young, but showed all onlookers how playful cities can be. The potential of this moment, the acute strangeness of the experience and the breaking down of the adult's barrier to living playfully, needs to be captured so the experience can be brought from the occasional festival into the mainstream fabric of our everyday streets, spaces and places. The temporary grassing over of Trafalgar Square[166] and of a street in the Methleys, Leeds,[167] and the creation of a public beach in Bristol* on a former car park,[168] all show the appetite for such positive challenges to the way we perceive and create cities.

Taking such moments seriously could yield valuable lessons for building a more successful city for children and young people, and therefore a successful city for everyone. Yet it will require a different way of shaping places, and one that recognises the wellbeing of children and young people as a crucial element of all place-shaping.

This last chapter outlines pathways to change. In doing so, it learns from the good (and bad) practice that was discovered in the six case studies. The aim is to realise the promise of the public realm for children and young people, and for everyone who uses it.

It is now widely recognised that the experiences of children and young people in public spaces are frequently negative. The impact is felt not just by individual children, but in the wider community as well. There are signals coming from policy as government attempts to tackle this situation. Three examples are new thinking on the role of streets as social spaces, public

---

* In the summer of 2007 Zero Zero and Demos helped Bristol to open its own urban beach; several of the photos in this report were taken on the Bristol Beach. As well as providing a place to relax, meet people and play, the project aimed to generate and share wider learning for other cities, policy-makers and practitioners.

space regeneration initiatives involving children as a resource rather than a nuisance, and the availability of Lottery money for improving play opportunities. Arguably the time has never been better to make positive changes.

Tangible and sustained improvements across the public realm cannot simply be delivered, nor can simple policy levers be pushed to 'drive through change'. Least of all can this happen solely via top-down initiatives and directives. Change must come from a much wider set of actors, including:

- policy-makers at local and national levels
- professionals whose work impacts on the built environment
- professionals working within the children and play sector
- parents, neighbours, friends and colleagues sharing responsibility for the climate of cultural attitudes towards children and young people.

Alignment

An important underpinning concept is alignment – a need to develop the recognition that the interests of children and the interests of the community at large are not opposed but closely aligned, and mutually dependent. Neighbourhood wellbeing cannot be achieved without truly inclusive and enjoyable facilities for children and young people. Town centres cannot be successfully regenerated if the needs and desires of children and young people are not listened to and acknowledged. Parks will not be welcoming for all if age segregation leads to conflict between different groups. Community engagement will miss out on vital insights if young people don't have a true voice. A reduction in child poverty will be less meaningful if the poverty of children's everyday experiences in public is not also addressed. And, ultimately, the government's ambitions for urban renaissance and sustainable communities will fail if children are not put at the heart of this agenda. The recommendations can be split into four themes:

- place-shaping
- collaborating across government
- co-producing spaces
- leadership and advocacy.

Place-shaping

Positive experiences for children don't depend just on particular playgrounds or services, they depend on the overall place offer to children and young people. This encompasses their myriad routes to school, the town centre and their local neighbourhood. Such sites are where their freedom, trust, confidence and agency have been most eroded, even though formal opportunities for involvement might have increased.

The place-shaping agenda forms a powerful tool for local governments to re-imagine our cities and focus on the wellbeing of an area and *all* its inhabitants. Local authorities and central government should harness the potential of this agenda for the benefit of children and young people.

• *Positive places:* 'Positive activities', such as those now advocated by government, are important, but the emphasis on structured youth provision should not eclipse the fact that children and young people have the right to be in public spaces in an informal and unorganised way too. The explicit recognition of the importance of having 'somewhere safe to hang out'[169] is vital and one that should not be overshadowed by the government's recent pledge of 'one youth centre in every town'. This *spatial* right needs to be recognised: the importance of the everyday public realm as a legitimate site for children and young people's informal recreation, and a dimension of wellbeing.

- *Beyond the playground*: The Big Lottery Fund's Children's Play Initiative provides welcome investment in play provision and has sent a clear message about the quantity and quality of places for play. However, the biggest gains for children and the public realm are yet to be made and lie outside the boundaries of dedicated play areas. The concept of playable space is powerful and asserts that play should be possible across the entire public realm (not just in playgrounds) and involve all generations (not just children). This concept needs to be embedded as an integral part of new street design and retrofitting urban redevelopment. This builds on the government's 'Manual for streets',[170] which establishes streets as social spaces, and the 2006 Planning Policy Statement on Housing which supported 'more family housing, including more play spaces, parks and gardens for children'.[171]

- *Traffic calming*: The dominance of car traffic is one of the greatest barriers to improved access to and use of the public realm. There are some quick wins to be made here. For example, the introduction of a 20 mph speed limit across all residential streets, as recently happened in Portsmouth,[172] would fundamentally re-shape how streets can be used and how they are perceived – benefiting not just children, but also wider community interaction and the environment.

- *Symbolic places for children*: Even though the emphasis in this pamphlet is firmly on everyday and shared spaces, the symbolism of places should not be forgotten. Hence there is a need to create a series of iconic play spaces in proximity to important tourist destinations, on central squares, and in high-profile new developments. Such a strategy could start with temporary installations to disrupt expectations of where play takes place.

Collaborating across government

The challenge of increased collaboration is a challenge of leaving professional silos behind, and finding a shared language and perspective on issues that don't fit neatly in one policy box or professional domain. In the context of the dispersed responsibility for public space a concerted effort to coordinate provision is essential.

- *Wellbeing comes first*: The emphasis on children and young people's wellbeing should facilitate a cross-cutting agenda which recognises the intertwined nature of place-shaping, children's and young people's services, and other fields such as health and the environment. On the national level, this realisation should become the core focus of the new, joint responsibility for play of the Department for Children, Schools and Families and the Department for Culture, Media and Sport, allowing them to explore innovative ways of collaborating with other departments (notably Communities and Local Government, the Department for Transport and the Department of Health) around children and place. Locally, children's and young people's services teams should champion the need for an inclusive public realm in local policy delivery. This should be a core element of local authority 'wellbeing' powers, as introduced in the Local Government Act 2000.[173]

- *Harnessing the potential of new policy structures*: The introduction of local area agreements and play strategies represents a huge opportunity for local authorities to raise the profile of children, establishing contacts and bringing together a range of issues, interests and disciplines to promote closer inter-departmental, inter-agency and cross-sectoral working. Designated champions with remit and responsibility to drive this collaborative working will be needed to make this happen at a practical level.

- *Better clients, better outcomes*: The commissioning phase of public realm improvement projects, from playgrounds to streetscape projects, is a crucial moment where alignment should occur. Collaborative brief-writing within local authorities, even for small projects, should involve experts from across the place-shaping sector, from landscape architects to transport planners and specialists. Similarly, local planning authorities should expect the same standards from private development as an integral part of the drive for better design standards.

- *Work swaps at all levels and all sectors*: One of the major problems identified in the research was the lack of shared language between the diverse professions. Interdisciplinary work experience would foster deeper understanding and could be aimed specifically at professionals who are most distanced from each other, for example swaps across transport and children's services or between green space management and the police.

Co-producing spaces

Some of the biggest challenges facing the state in the coming years cannot be solved by central government alone: climate change, the obesity crisis and the care deficit are only a few examples. They demand a much more interactive relationship between the individual and the state. As a response to these kinds of issues the idea of co-production has gained currency over recent years at least in relation to the design and delivery of public services for adults. There is scope for extending it to children and young people.

- *Recognise children's and young people's agency beyond the playground*: Asking for children's and young people's input for the next playground or youth facility is important, but only goes so far if the real causes of their frustration lie elsewhere. Regeneration and public realm projects almost always affect young people, and their voice in the formal consultation processes should be enhanced. The role of 'young advisors' to 'youth proof' policies, development proposals and strategies is one good example of how this can be taken forward.

- *Collaborative place audits and intergenerational projects*: Children and adults often have similar basic complaints about spaces. Collaborative place audits, which investigate local public realm qualities and deficits in a structured manner, can provide forums for local discussion and identify areas in need of investment. The benefits reach beyond physical improvements and can help change perceptions between adults and young people.

- *Devolve power to encourage local innovation*: The government's double devolution drive promises the handing down of power to the public. The potential of this agenda should be explored to the full to encourage local innovation such as neighbourhood play toolkits, local budgeting and community asset transfers that benefit multiple generations.

- *Developing local capacity for engagement*: Many place-shaping professionals admit that they lack the skills and capacity for greater engagement with children and young people. These deficits need to be addressed to increase awareness and confidence in consulting and working with young people, seeing them as partners in the place-shaping process, and shaping shared understanding of spaces and places.

- *Develop the role of intermediaries*: It is not always possible to 'access' young people directly; often, an understanding and acknowledgement of trusted networks is key. Members of the community and local services (youth workers, teachers, play rangers etc) are key intermediaries and play a vital role in connecting place-shapers with children, filling that 'empty space' between parents, society and the police. The potential of the voluntary and community sector to maximise its contribution to place improvement should be recognised and resourced.

Leadership and advocacy

There is a duty of care in governance for young people. Moving away from the 'landscape of powerlessness' that children and young people experience means more than formally involving them in decision-making. We need to accept that adults – place-shaping professionals, politicians and the wider public – all bear some responsibility for children's experiences in public spaces.

- *The importance of professional organisations*: The role of professional organisations should be to encourage more collaborative practice, alongside developing a sophisticated understanding of how their profession impacts on children and young people. From architects to police organisations, from landscape designers to traffic planners, town centre managers to planners, such organisations need to expand their scope beyond traditional core business to arrive at more holistic place-making practice.

- *Political leadership*: Point-scoring by being tough on children and youth might be politically expedient but it does little to get beyond the current stand-off. Instead, recognising how children and young people's wellbeing is deeply intertwined with wider community concerns and policy agendas such as crime reduction, good governance and sustainability will provide a more positive agenda for action.

- *Pointing the finger back*: An anti-social behaviour hotline targeted at adults, through which children and young people can report anti-social behaviour of adults towards their legitimate right to be and play outside, could become a major campaigning tool to be added to successful initiatives such as Playday to advocate children's and young people's right to be in public space.

- *Collaboration for play – beyond the play sector*: The biggest gain for the play sector lies in increased collaboration with other advocacy organisations for change in the public realm, such as those advocating sustainable transport modes, traffic safety and pedestrian campaigns, elderly and disabled access movements, and those promoting and delivering sport and community events in local streets, influencing the movers and shapers for the benefit of frontline delivery.

There are plenty of reasons to be optimistic about the future of children and the public realm: there is a wealth of ideas, initiatives, good will and good practice around the country. The recommendations set out here aim to find ways of building on this energy. Together they are offered as a set of provocations and first steps to re-imagining the public spaces in our cities, towns and villages and how they might work better for children and young people.

In doing so, we have chosen not to emphasise the elimination of the 'bads' from children's lives. The banning of advertising to children might be useful, but does not represent a new way forward or create value for children. Similarly an overemphasis on risks, threats and children being 'out of control' impoverishes our ability to talk about and with children. We need to start a different kind of conversation where children are not just vulnerable but also vocal and active agents of their own lives and the places where they live.

The vision sketched out in this pamphlet makes a conscious challenge to those who design, build and manage the built environment as no more than the sum of functionalist requirements: from work, housing and movement to shopping. Children will benefit if the public realm is understood as a shared resource and site of exchange, interaction and collective experiences. Playable space, and playful streets that are welcoming to all generations, should be the normative vision guiding the ambitions for urban renaissance and sustainable communities. This is a call to policy-makers and those on the frontline of place-shaping alike. If this call is taken seriously, all will benefit.

Appendix 1

List of attendees at the project sounding board meeting January 2007

Anne-Marie Andreoli	Department for Culture, Media and Sport
Issy Cole-Hamilton	Play England
Nicole Collomb	CABE Space
Lisa Davis	Play England
Patricia Durr	Children's Society
Paul Durr	Play England
Michael Follett	South Gloucestershire Council
Matthew Frith	Peabody Trust
Tim Gill	Independent consultant and writer on childhood
Ashley Godfrey	Play England consultant
Phil Heaton	Parklife Ltd
Lauren Lacey	Play England
Tony Leach	London Parks and Green Spaces Forum
Sue Morgan	Around the Block Ltd
Tim Pope	Communities and Local Government
Helen Woolley	University of Sheffield
Ken Worpole	Writer and environmentalist

List of attendees at the place-shapers forum May 2007

Caroline Abrahams	Local Government Association
Cany Ash	Ash Sakula Architects
Dominic Church	Commission for Architecture and the Built Environment
Tim Gill	Independent consultant and writer on childhood
Phil Heaton	Parklife Ltd
Annabel Hodges	Alan Baxter & Associates
Liz Kessler	EC1 New Deal for Communities
Tom Landell Mills	Groundwork Camden & Islington
Tony Leach	London Parks and Green Spaces Forum
Sue Morgan	Around the Block Ltd

Safia Noor	Greater London Authority
Adrian Pigott	London Borough of Brent – Transportation
Carolyn Robertson	Age Concern
Nathaniel Roberton	London Borough of Haringey – Planning
Jim Trotman	Thames Valley Police
Judith Walker	Institute of Highway Incorporated Engineers
Adam White	Groundwork UK Federation
Anna Whitworth	Communities and Local Government

Appendix 2

Expert interviews

Anne Marie Andreoli	Department for Culture, Media and Sport (20 Dec 2006)
June Barnes	East Thames Group Housing Association (30 May 2007)
Caroline Boswell	Greater London Authority (10 Nov 2006)
Michael Follet	South Gloucestershire Council (13 Dec 2006)
Tim Gill	Independent consultant and writer on childhood (5 Dec 2006)
Roger Hart	University of New York (20 Nov 2006)
Richard Hebditch	Living Streets (7 Dec 2006)
Esther Hughes	Children's Society / Good Childhood Enquiry (15 Dec 2006)
Chris Jenks	Brunel University (22 Nov 2006)
Owain Jones	University of Exeter (23 Nov 2006)
Peter Lipman	Sustrans (8 Dec 2006)
Roger Mackett	University College London (24 Nov 2006)
Denise Maguire	Department for Transport (30 May 2007)
Lamine Mahdjoubi	University of West of England (8 Dec 2006)
Hugh Matthews	University of Northampton (26 Jan 2007)
Berry Mayall	University of London (29 Nov 2006)
Ute Navidi	London Play (11 Jan 2007)
Tim Pope	Communities and Local Government (4 Dec 2006)
Bernard Spiegal	Playlink (9 Mar 2007)
Helen Woolley	University of Sheffield (1 Dec 2006)

Notes

1   Latest figures show a dramatic
      reduction in children playing
      in their local streets, Play
      England, see www.playengland.
      org.uk/Page.asp?originx_
      5589tx_93461909704922t80w_
      20077305256b (accessed
      6 Aug 2007).

2   L Clark, '"Out-of-control" British
      teens the worst behaved in Europe',
      Daily Mail, 26 Jul 2007, see www.
      dailymail.co.uk/pages/live/articles/
      news/news.html?in_article_
      id=470919&in_page_id=1770
      (accessed 6 Aug 2007).

3   B Fenton, 'Junk culture "is
      poisoning our children"', *Telegraph.
      co.uk*, see www.telegraph.
      co.uk/news/main.jhtml?xml=/
      news/2006/09/12/njunk12.
      xml (accessed 12 Aug 2007); S
      Palmer, *Toxic Childhood* (London:
      Orion Publishers, 2006).

4   P Wilby, 'Britain has lost the art of
      socializing the young', *Guardian*, 1
      Aug 2007, see www.guardian.co.uk/
      commentisfree/story/0,,2138842,00.
      html (accessed 6 Aug 2007).

5   See *Make Space Youth Review*
      (London: 4Children, 2007),
      available at www.4children.org.
      uk/information/show/ref/1020
      (accessed 6 Aug 2007).

6   E Leigh, quoted in 'Yobs make city
      centres "no-go areas"', *Independent*,
      24 Jul 2007, available at http://news.
      independent.co.uk/uk/politics/
      article2795752.ece (accessed

      14 Aug 2007); see also Public
      Accounts Committee, 'Tackling
      anti-social behaviour', 24 Jul 2007,
      available at www.publications.
      parliament.uk/pa/cm200607/
      cmselect/cmpubacc/246/246.
      pdf (accessed 14 Aug 2007).

7   Unicef Innocenti Research Centre,
      *Child Poverty in Perspective: An
      overview of child well-being in rich
      countries* (Florence: Unicef, 2007).

8   'UK is accused of failing
      children', see http://news.
      bbc.co.uk/1/hi/uk/6359363.
      stm (accessed 6 Aug 2007).

9   'Government misses poverty
      target', available at http://news.bbc.
      co.uk/1/hi/uk_politics/4788270.
      stm (accessed 12 Aug 2007).

10   The new Secretary of State for
      Children, Schools and Families,
      Ed Balls, affirmed the new
      government's commitment to play,
      stating that 'Childhood is a time for
      learning and exploring. Through
      playing and doing positive activities,
      children and young people can
      learn to better understand the
      opportunities and challenges in the
      world around them, and how to be
      safe.' See 'Consultation launched on
      helping children and young people
      stay safe', 18 Jul 2007, available
      at www.everychildmatters.gov.
      uk/news/?asset=News&id=71119
      (accessed 14 Aug 2007).

11   See www.playengland.org.
      uk/Page.asp?originx6296tn_34

181211460913h40d9245014801 (accessed 6 Aug 2007).

12 The 'Mosquito' is a device that emits a high-pitched noise audible only to young people under the age of 25, irritating enough to make them go elsewhere but not damaging to their ears. Staffordshire Police's website claimed in 2006 that the 'sonic teenage deterrent' had helped to move on 'nuisance youths' from outside shops, where other traditional dispersal methods had failed. See 'Mosquito moves on nuisance youths', *Staffordshire Police News*, 15 Feb 2006, www.staffordshire.police. uk/news/2006/02_feb/15_mosquito. htm (accessed 6 Aug 2007).

13 The Children's Society, *Good Childhood? A question for our time*, the Good Childhood national inquiry launch report (London: Children's Society, 2006).

14 Plato, *The Laws* (London: Penguin, 2005).

15 See www.ohchr.org/english/law/crc. htm (accessed 14 Aug 2007).

16 Quoted in HM Treasury and Department for Education and Skills, *Children and Young People's Review – Evidence from the Children's Play Council*, 15 Sep 2006, see www.hm-treasury.gov. uk/media/B/0/cypreview2006_ childrensplaycouncil1.pdf (accessed 9 Aug 2007).

17 D Massey, *For Space* (London: Sage, 2005).

18 Commission for Architecture and the Built Environment, *The Value of Public Space* (London: CABE, 2004), available at www. cabe.org.uk/default.aspx?conte ntitemid=475&field=browse_su bject&term=Public%20space&t ype=2 (accessed 6 Aug 2007).

19 J Jacobs, *The Death and Life of Great American Cities* (New York: Random House and Vintage Books, 1961).

20 I Cole-Hamilton, A Harrop and C Street, *The Value of Children's Play and Play Provision: A systematic review of the literature* (London: New Policy Institute, 2002), see www.npi.org. uk/reports/play%20literature. pdf (accessed 13 Aug 2007).

21 G Thomas and G Hocking, *Other People's Children: Why their quality of life is our concern* (London: Demos, 2003).

22 Department of Health, *At Least Five a Week: Evidence on the impact of physical activity and its relationship to health* (London: DoH, 2004).

23 R Mackett, *Making Children's Lives More Active* (London: Centre for Transport Studies, University College London, 2004), see www. cts.ucl.ac.uk/research/chcaruse/ trandh87.pdf (accessed 6 Aug 2007).

24 C Rogers and J Sawyer, *Play in the Lives of Children* (Washington: National Association for the Education of Young Children, 1988).

25 M Hillman, J Adams and N Whitelegg, *One False Move: A study of children's independent mobility* (London: Policy Studies Institute, 1990).

26 Play England, *Planning for Play: Guidance on the development of play strategies* (London: National Children's Bureau / Big Lottery Fund, 2006), see www.playengland.

org.uk/downloads/pdf/planning_
for_play.pdf (accessed 7 Aug 2007).

27 J Santer, C Griffiths and D Goodall,
Free Play in Early Childhood: A
literature review (London: National
Children's Bureau, 2007).

28 R Sennett, The Fall of Public Man
(London: Penguin, 1991).

29 F Coalter and J Taylor, Realising
the Potential of Cultural Services:
The case for play (London:
Local Government Association,
2001), available at www.lga.
gov.uk/Documents/Briefing/
Our_Work/culture/play.pdf
(accessed 7 Aug 2007).

30 E Adams and S Ingham, Changing
Places: Children's participation in
environmental planning (London:
Children's Society, 1998); M Jans,
'Children as citizens: towards a
contemporary notion of child
participation', Childhood 11 (2004).

31 Adams and Ingham,
Changing Places.

32 G Thomas and G Thompson, A
Child's Place (London: Demos
/ Green Alliance, 2004).

33 K Worpole and K Knox, The
Social Value of Public Places
(York: Joseph Rowntree
Foundation, 2007), see www.jrf.
org.uk/bookshop/eBooks/2050-
public-space-community.
pdf (accessed 7 Aug 2007).

34 C Ward, The Child in the City (New
York: Pantheon Books, 1978).

35 D Appleyard, Livable Streets
(Berkeley: University of
California Press, 1982).

36 H Kapasi, Neighbourhood Play and
Community Action (York: Joseph
Rowntree Foundation, 2006).

37 A Buonfino and P Hilder,

Neighbouring in Contemporary
Britain: A think-piece for the Joseph
Rowntree Foundation Housing and
Neighbourhoods Committee (York /
London: JRF / Young Foundation,
2006); A Park et al, British
Social Attitudes: The 23rd report:
Perspectives on a changing society
(London: Sage Publications, 2007).

38 J Margo et al, Freedom's Orphans:
Raising youth in a changing
world (London: Institute for
Public Policy Research, 2006).

39 Kapasi, Neighbourhood Play
and Community Action.

40 P Kane, 'Play for today',
Observer, 22 Oct 2000, see
http://observer.guardian.co.uk/
life/story/0,6903,386013,00.
html (accessed 6 Aug 2007).

41 J Huizinga, Homo Ludens
(Boston: Beacon Press, 1971).

42 P Kane, 'Play for today'.

43 P Kane, The Play Ethic: A manifesto
for a different way of living
(London: Macmillan, 2004).

44 L Lefenbre and I de Roode (eds),
Aldo van Eijk: The playgrounds
and the city (Amsterdam /
Rotterdam: Stedelijk Museum
/ NAI Publishers, 2002).

45 E Penalosa and S Ives, 'The
politics of happiness', Yes
Magazine, Summer 2003, see
http://yesmagazine.org/article.
asp?id=615 (accessed 9 Aug 2007).

46 Demos interview, 2 May 2007.

47 K Worpole, No Particular Place
to Go: Children, young people
and public space (Birmingham:
Groundwork, 2003), www.
groundwork.org.uk/upload/
publications/publication6.
pdf (accessed 7 Aug 2007).

48   A Hastings et al, 'Cleaning up neighbourhoods: environmental problems and service provision in deprived neighbourhoods', see www.jrf.org.uk/knowledge/findings/housing/0515.asp (accessed 6 Aug 2007).

49   'Deprived areas "fed up with mess"', *BBCnews.co.uk*, 1 Nov 2005, available at http://news.bbc.co.uk/1/hi/scotland/4393284.stm (accessed 19 Jun 2007).

50   T Grayling et al, *Streets Ahead: Safe and liveable streets for children* (London: ippr and Imperial College Centre for Transport Studies, 2002).

51   M Hillman (ed), *Children, Transport and the Quality of Life* (London: Policy Studies Institute, 1993).

52   Department of Transport, Local Government and Regions, *Improving Urban Parks, Play Areas and Open Spaces*, Urban Research Report (London: DTLR, May 2002).

53   Quoted in I Cole-Hamilton, *Developing Models for Sustainable Play Provision* (London: National Children's Bureau, 2006).

54   D McNeish and H Roberts, *Playing It Safe: Today's children at play* (Ilford: Barnardo's, 1995), quoted in Cole-Hamilton et al, *The Value of Children's Play and Play Provision*.

55   Ibid.

56   Department of Health, *Choosing Health: Making healthy choices easier*, Public Health white paper (London: DoH, 2004), quoted in B Manwaring and C Taylor, 'The benefits of play and playwork: recent evidence-based research (2001–2006) demonstrating the impact and benefits of play and playwork', available at www.skillsactive.com/resources/research/CYWU_Research_Complete.pdf (accessed 6 Aug 2007).

57   Cited in Worpole, *No Particular Place to Go*.

58   Unicef Innocenti Research Centre, *Child Poverty in Perspective*.

59   WH Dietz, 'Reduce television viewing and promote playing', *British Medical Journal* 322 (10 Feb 2001), see www.bmj.com/cgi/content/full/322/7282/313 (accessed 6 Aug 2007).

60   DJL Kuh and C Cooper, 'Physical activity at 36 years: patterns and childhood predictors in a longitudinal study', *Journal of Epidemiology and Community Health* 46 (1992).

61   National Audit Office, Healthcare Commission and Audit Commission, *Tackling Child Obesity: First steps* (London: NAO, Healthcare Commission and Audit Commission, 2006).

62   Quoted in Manwaring and Taylor, 'The benefits of play and playwork'. For more on 'play deprivation' see B Hughes, 'Play deprivation, play bias and playwork practice' in F Brown (ed), *Playwork Theory and Practice* (Maidenhead, Berks: Open University Press, 2003).

63   SL Brown, 'Play as an organising principle: clinical evidence and personal observations' in M Bekoff and JA Byers (eds), *Animal Play: Evolutionary, comparative and ethological perspectives* (Cambridge: Cambridge University Press, 1998).

64   See www.crimereduction.gov.uk/asbos/asbos2.htm (accessed 16 Jul 2007).

65   'Never mind crime, tidy up the

garden: an area's "liveability" is best guide to locals' happiness, says report', *Guardian*, 24 Jun 2005; B Page and E Wallace, *Families, Children and Young People: Key issues* (London: Ipsos MORI, Mar 2004), see www.ipsos-mori. com/publications/bp/families-key-issues.pdf (accessed 15 Aug 2007).

66   Ipsos MORI, 'Public concern about ASB and support for ASBOs', available at www.ipsos-mori.com/polls/2005/asbo-top. shtml (accessed 16 Jul 2007).

67   See Play Wales website at www. playwales.org.uk/page.asp?id=51 (accessed 15 Aug 2007).

68   S Lipton, 'Better public spaces', *New Statesman*, 24 Mar 2003, see www.newstatesman. com/pdf/publicspacesupp. pdf (accessed 1 Aug 2007).

69   S Johnson, 'Theme-parking the American city (Welcome to the Pleasure Dome)', *Village Voice Literary Supplement* (Feb–March 1999), 16 Feb 1999.

70   Demos interview, 27 Apr 2007.

71   Demos interview, 26 Apr 2007.

72   See www.homezonenews.org. uk/ (accessed 14 Aug 2007).

73   See www.neighbourhood. gov.uk/page.asp?id=633 (accessed 6 Aug 2007).

74   R Rogers, *Towards a Strong Urban Renaissance: An independent report by members of the Urban Task Force*, chaired by Lord Rogers of Riverside, available at www. urbantaskforce.org/UTF_final_ report.pdf (accessed 6 Aug 2007).

75   Land Registry, House Price Index, April 2007, available at www.landregistry.gov.uk/assets/ library/documents/hpir0507. pdf (accessed 4 Jul 2007).

76   'Residential land prices significantly outstrip house price growth', HBOS plc, 2003, available at www. hbosplc.com/media/pressreleases/ articles/halifax/2003/land_prices_ outstrip_house_price_growth. doc (accessed 4 Jul 2007).

77   D MacLeod, 'Association calculates "shameful" loss of playing fields', *Guardian*, 1 Aug 2005, see http://education.guardian.co.uk/ schoolsports/story/0,,1540439,00. html (accessed 6 Aug 2007).

78   Demos interview, 30 May 2007.

79   H Cope, *Capital Gains Making High Density Housing Work in London* (London: London Housing Federation, 2002).

80   Thomas and Thompson, *A Child's Place.*

81   Demos interview, 11 Apr 2007.

82   Demos interview, 12 Apr 2007.

83   *Public Park Assessment: A survey of local authority owned parks focusing on parks of historic interest*, Urban Parks Forum, May 2001, executive summary available at www.green-space.org.uk/whatwedo/ppa. php (accessed 6 Aug 2007).

84   'Local authority historic parks in the UK', *Cultural Trends* 38, Policy Studies Institute (2000).

85   See www.publications.parliament. uk/pa/cm200203/cmselect/ cmodpm/673/67309.htm (accessed 13 Aug 2007) and www. renewal.net/Documents/RNET/ Research/Literaturereviewpublic. pdf (accessed 9 Aug 2007).

86   CABE's housing audit 2005: 93 schemes by the ten largest-volume housebuilders in the

north east, north west, Yorkshire and Humber, see www.cabe. org.uk/AssetLibrary/173. pdf (accessed 6 Aug 2007).

87 Demos interview, 26 Apr 2007.

88 CABE, 'Living with risk: promoting better public space design', Jul 2007, available at www.cabe.org.uk/ default.aspx?contentitemid=1930 (accessed 6 Aug 2007).

89 Demos interview, 8 Dec 2006.

90 'Play, participation and potential', available at www. groundwork.org.uk/upload/ publications/publication11. pdf (accessed 9 Aug 2007).

91 Department for Transport, 'Vehicle licensing statistics: 2006', see www.dft.gov.uk/pgr/ statistics/datatablespublications/ vehicles/licensing/ vehiclelicensingstatistics2006 (accessed 6 Aug 2007).

92 Census 2001, see www.statistics. gov.uk/CCI/nugget.asp?ID=348 &Pos=2&ColRank=1&Rank=310 (accessed 6 Aug 2007).

93 'Latest figures show dramatic reduction in children playing in their local streets', 30 Jul 2007, see www.playengland. org.uk/Page.asp?originx_ 5589tx_93461909704922t80w_ 20077305256b (accessed 6 Aug 2007).

94 See www.homezonenews.org. uk/ (accessed 12 Jun 2007); and www.londonplay.org.uk/ document.php?document_id=478 (accessed 2 Aug 2007).

95 Demos interview, 26 Apr 2007.

96 Demos interview, 27 Apr 2007.

97 Demos interview, 27 Apr 2007.

98 See M Hillman, 'Introduction: more

restrictions, more trouble ahead', in S Waiton, Scared of the Kids? Curfews, crime and the regulation of young people (Sheffield: Sheffield Hallam University Press, 2001).

99 Rogers, Towards a Strong Urban Renaissance.

100 See Communities and Local Government, Planning Policy Statement 6: Planning for town centres (Norwich, HMSO, 2005), available at www.communities. gov.uk/index.asp?id=1143820 (accessed 14 Aug 2007).

101 H Woolley and R Johns, 'Skateboarding: the city as a playground', Journal of Urban Design 6, no 2 (1 Jun 2001).

102 I Johar, 'Public space is dead; long live public space' in J Beunderman et al, BCN–LDN 2020 (Barcelona: Fundació Ramon Trias Fargas, 2007).

103 C Spencer and H Woolley, 'Children and the city: a summary of recent environmental psychology research', Child Care, Health and Development 26, no 3 (2000).

104 Demos interview, 8 Dec 2006.

105 Quoted in G Valentine, 'Oh yes I can.' 'Oh no you can't.': children and parents' understandings of kids' competence to negotiate public space safely, Antipode 29, no 1 (Jan 1997).

106 Ibid. See also A James, C Jenks and A Prout, Theorizing Childhood (Cambridge: Polity Press, 1998).

107 As Chris Jenks writes in James et al, Theorizing Childhood, 'the modern child's relationship to the city finds them as "a victim of public space"'.

108 Demos interview, 26 Apr 2007.

109 Demos interview, 2 May 2007.

110 See http://news.bbc.co.uk/1/
hi/talking_point/981385.stm
(accessed 13 Aug 2007).
111 Ward, *Child in the City*, citing I Opie
and P Opie, *Children's Games in the
Streets and Playground* (Oxford:
Oxford University Press, 1969).
112 S Nicholas, C Kershaw and
A Walker (eds), *Crime in
England and Wales 2006/2007*,
2007, see www.homeoffice.
gov.uk/rds/pdfs07/hosb1107.
pdf (accessed 14 Aug 2007).
113 'Respect? The voice behind the
hood: young people's views on
anti-social behaviour, the media
and older people', YouthNet and
the British Youth Council, Jul
2006, available at www.youthnet.
org/content/1/c6/02/80/36/
Respect%20report%20final.
pdf (accessed 27 Jul 2007).
114 Demos interview, 3 May 2007.
115 Demos interview, 26 Apr 2007.
116 Demos interview, 27 Apr 2007.
117 Home Office, *The Respect Action
Plan* (London: Home Office, 2006),
available at www.homeoffice.gov.
uk/documents/respect-action-
plan (accessed 7 Aug 2007).
118 HM Treasury, *Aiming High for Young
People: A 10 year strategy for positive
activities* (London: HM Treasury,
Jul 2007), see www.hm-treasury.gov.
uk/spending_review/spend_csr07/
reviews/cyp_review/cypreview_
index.cfm (accessed 27 Jul 2007).
119 'ASBOs mean failure, says
minister', *BBC.co.uk*, 27 Jul
2007, see http://news.bbc.
co.uk/1/hi/uk_politics/6918664.
stm (accessed 7 Aug 2007).
120 See www.communities.gov.
uk/index.asp?id=1502424

(accessed 13 Aug 2007).
121 ippr, *Freedom's Orphans*
(London: ippr, Nov 2006).
122 Demos interview, 25 Apr 2007.
123 L Trilling, *A Gathering of Fugitives*
(London: Secker & Warburg, 1957).
124 Palmer, *Toxic Childhood*.
125 McNeish and Roberts,
Playing It Safe.
126 Unicef *A League Table of Child
Deaths by Injury in Rich Nations*,
Innocenti Report Card, no 2
(Florence: Unicef, Feb 2001).
127 Ward, *Child in the City*.
128 Thomas and Hocking,
Other People's Children.
129 Unicef Innocenti Research Centre,
Child Poverty in Perspective.
130 'No playground for "super
school"', *BBC.co.uk*, 6 May 2007,
see http://news.bbc.co.uk/1/hi/
england/cambridgeshire/6629655.
stm (accessed 8 Aug 2007).
131 Demos interview, 19 Apr 2007.
132 See www.idea.gov.uk/idk/
core/page.do?pageId=5595018
(accessed 13 Aug 2007).
133 Department of Communities
and Local Government, *Planning
for a Sustainable Future*, white
paper, Cm 7120 (Norwich,
HMSO, May 2007), available
at www.communities.gov.uk/
embedded_object.asp?id=1510669
(accessed 14 Aug 2007).
134 Demos interview, 10 May 2007.
135 J Craig, 'Production values:
building shared autonomy' in J
Craig (ed), *Production Values:
Futures for professionalism*
(London: Demos, 2006).
136 Demos interview, 24 Apr 2007.
137 A Davis and L Jones, 'Whose
neighbourhood? Whose quality

of life? Developing a new agenda for children's health in urban settings', *Health Education Journal* 56, no 4 (1997).

138 See Communities and Local Government, *Planning Policy Statement 6*.

139 See Ruth Kelly's 'Foreword' to DfES, *Youth Matters*, green paper, Jul 2005, available at www.dfes.gov.uk/publications/youth/fore.shtml (accessed 13 Aug 2007).

140 H Matthews and M Limb, 'Another white elephant? Youth councils as democratic structures', *Space and Polity* 7, no 2 (Aug 2003).

141 P Skidmore, K Bound and H Lownsbrough, *Community Participation: Who benefits?* (York: Joseph Rowntree Foundation, 2006).

142 Ipsos MORI, 'Young people "feel excluded from decisions"', 13 Jul 2006, see www.ipsos-mori.com/polls/2006/occ.shtml (accessed 6 Aug 2007).

143 Demos interview, 2 May 2007.

144 Demos interview, 10 Apr 2007.

145 Demos interview, 19 Apr 2007.

146 Demos interview, 3 May 2007.

147 Demos interview, 3 May 2007.

148 Demos interview, 11 Apr 2007.

149 Demos interview, 12 Apr 2007.

150 Demos interview, 12 Apr 2007.

151 Quoted in Groundwork, *A Play Strategy for Derbyshire Dales*, available at www.derbyshiredales.gov.uk/NR/rdonlyres/B2D600CA-F7C2-4FB5-8E25-0847C77DE714/0/DraftPlayStrategy.pdf (accessed 13 Aug 2007).

152 Play England, *Planning for Play*.

153 Demos interview, 3 May 2007.

154 Demos interview, 26 Apr 2007.

155 Demos interview, 3 May 2007.

156 Demos interview, 10 May 2007.

157 Demos interview, 26 Mar 2007.

158 See FLUID architects, 'Your place or mine?' in P Blundell-Jones, D Petrescu and J Till (eds), *Architecture and Participation* (London: Routledge, 2005).

159 Demos interview, 10 May 2007.

160 Demos interview, 10 Apr 2007.

161 Demos interview, 2 May 2007.

162 Demos interview, 3 May 2007.

163 Demos interview, 26 Mar 2007.

164 Demos interview, 10 Apr 2007.

165 Demos interview, 26 Mar 2007.

166 http://news.bbc.co.uk/1/hi/england/london/6687089.stm (accessed 13 Aug 2007).

167 Tony Harcup, 'Re-imaging a post-industrial city: the Leeds St Valentine's Fair as a civic spectacle', *City: Analysis of urban trends, culture, theory, policy, action* 4, no 2 (1 Jul 2000).

168 See www.demos.co.uk/projects/bristolurbanbeach/overview (accessed 14 Aug 2007).

169 See *Youth Matters* (Norwich, HMSO, 2005), available at www.dfes.gov.uk/publications/youth/docs/youthmatters.pdf (accessed 13 Aug 2007).

170 See www.manualforstreets.org.uk/ (accessed 15 Aug 2007).

171 Communities and Local Government, 'PPS3: Delivering the family and affordable homes communities need', news release 2006/0158, Nov 2006, www.communities.gov.uk/index.asp?id=1002882&PressNoticeID=2304 (accessed 15 Aug 2007).

172 www.portsmouth.gov.uk/living/8403.html (accessed 13 Aug 2007).

173 See www.opsi.gov.uk/Acts/

DEM☉S

1. Definitions

a "Collective Work" means a work, such as a periodical issue, anthology or encyclopedia, in which the Work in its entirety in unmodified form, along with a number of other contributions, constituting separate and independent works in themselves, are assembled into a collective whole. A work that constitutes a Collective Work will not be considered a Derivative Work (as defined below) for the purposes of this Licence.

b "Derivative Work" means a work based upon the Work or upon the Work and other pre-existing works, such as a musical arrangement, dramatization, fictionalization, motion picture version, sound recording, art reproduction, abridgment, condensation, or any other form in which the Work may be recast, transformed, or adapted, except that a work that constitutes a Collective Work or a translation from English into another language will not be considered a Derivative Work for the purpose of this Licence.

c "Licensor" means the individual or entity that offers the Work under the terms of this Licence.

d "Original Author" means the individual or entity who created the Work.

e "Work" means the copyrightable work of authorship offered under the terms of this Licence.

f "You" means an individual or entity exercising rights under this Licence who has not previously violated the terms of this Licence with respect to the Work,or who has received express permission from DEMOS to exercise rights under this Licence despite a previous violation.

2. Fair Use Rights.

Nothing in this licence is intended to reduce, limit, or restrict any rights arising from fair use, first sale or other limitations on the exclusive rights of the copyright owner under copyright law or other applicable laws.

3. Licence Grant.

Subject to the terms and conditions of this Licence, Licensor hereby grants You a worldwide, royalty-free, non-exclusive,perpetual (for the duration of the applicable copyright) licence to exercise the rights in the Work as stated below:

a to reproduce the Work, to incorporate the Work into one or more Collective Works, and to reproduce the Work as incorporated in the Collective Works;

b to distribute copies or phonorecords of, display publicly,perform publicly, and perform publicly by means of a digital audio transmission the Work including as incorporated in Collective Works;

The above rights may be exercised in all media and formats whether now known or hereafter devised.The above rights include the right to make such modifications as are technically necessary to exercise the rights in other media and formats. All rights not expressly granted by Licensor are hereby reserved.

4. Restrictions.

The licence granted in Section 3 above is expressly made subject to and limited by the following restrictions:

a You may distribute,publicly display, publicly perform, or publicly digitally perform the Work only under the terms of this Licence, and You must include a copy of, or the Uniform Resource Identifier for, this Licence with every copy or phonorecord of the Work You distribute, publicly display,publicly perform, or publicly digitally perform. You may not offer or impose any terms on the Work that alter or restrict the terms of this Licence or the recipients' exercise of the rights granted hereunder.You may not sublicence the Work.You must keep intact all notices that refer to this Licence and to the disclaimer of warranties.You may not distribute, publicly display, publicly perform, or publicly digitally perform the Work with any technological measures that control access or use of the Work in a manner inconsistent with the terms of this Licence Agreement.The above applies to the Work as incorporated in a Collective Work, but this does not require the Collective Work apart from the Work itself to be made subject to the terms of this Licence. If You create a Collective Work, upon notice from any Licencor You must, to the extent practicable, remove from the Collective Work any reference to such Licensor or the Original Author, as requested.

b You may not exercise any of the rights granted to You in Section 3 above in any manner that is primarily intended for or directed toward commercial advantage or private monetary compensation.The exchange of the Work for other copyrighted works by means of digital filesharing or otherwise shall not be considered to be intended for or directed toward commercial advantage or private monetary compensation, provided there is no payment of any monetary compensation in connection with the exchange of copyrighted works.

c If you distribute, publicly display, publicly perform, or publicly digitally perform the Work or ny Collective Works,You must keep intact all copyright notices for the Work and give the Original Author credit reasonable to the medium or means You are utilizing by conveying the name (or pseudonym if applicable) of the Original Author if supplied; the title of the Work if supplied. Such credit may be implemented in any reasonable manner; provided, however, that in the case of a Collective Work, at a minimum such credit will appear where any other comparable authorship credit appears and in a manner at least as prominent as such other comparable authorship credit.

5. Representations,Warranties and Disclaimer

a By offering the Work for public release under this Licence, Licensor represents and warrants that, to the best of Licensor's knowledge after reasonable inquiry:

i Licensor has secured all rights in the Work necessary to grant the licence rights hereunder and to permit the lawful exercise of the rights granted hereunder without You having any obligation to pay any royalties, compulsory licence fees, residuals or any other payments;

ii The Work does not infringe the copyright, trademark, publicity rights, common law rights or any other right of any third party or constitute defamation, invasion of privacy or other tortious injury to any third party.

b EXCEPT AS EXPRESSLY STATED IN THIS LICENCE OR OTHERWISE AGREED IN WRITING OR REQUIRED BY APPLICABLE LAW,THE WORK IS LICENCED ON AN "AS IS"BASIS,WITHOUT WARRANTIES OF ANY KIND, EITHER EXPRESS OR IMPLIED INCLUDING,WITHOUT LIMITATION,ANY WARRANTIES REGARDING THE CONTENTS OR ACCURACY OF THE WORK.

6. Limitation on Liability.

EXCEPT TO THE EXTENT REQUIRED BY APPLICABLE LAW, AND EXCEPT FOR DAMAGES ARISING FROM LIABILITY TO A THIRD PARTY RESULTING FROM BREACH OF THE WARRANTIES IN SECTION 5, IN NO EVENT WILL

LICENSOR BE LIABLE TO YOU ON ANY LEGAL THEORY FOR ANY SPECIAL, INCIDENTAL,CONSEQUENTIAL, PUNITIVE OR EXEMPLARY DAMAGES ARISING OUT OF THIS LICENCE OR THE USE OF THE WORK, EVEN IF LICENSOR HAS BEEN ADVISED OF THE POSSIBILITY OF SUCH DAMAGES.

7. Termination

a This Licence and the rights granted hereunder will terminate automatically upon any breach by You of the terms of this Licence. Individuals or entities who have received Collective Works from You under this Licence,however, will not have their licences terminated provided such individuals or entities remain in full compliance with those licences. Sections 1, 2, 5, 6, 7, and 8 will survive any termination of this Licence.

b Subject to the above terms and conditions, the licence granted here is perpetual (for the duration of the applicable copyright in the Work). Notwithstanding the above, Licensor reserves the right to release the Work under different licence terms or to stop distributing the Work at any time; provided, however that any such election will not serve to withdraw this Licence (or any other licence that has been, or is required to be, granted under the terms of this Licence), and this Licence will continue in full force and effect unless terminated as stated above.

8. Miscellaneous

a Each time You distribute or publicly digitally perform the Work or a Collective Work, DEMOS offers to the recipient a licence to the Work on the same terms and conditions as the licence granted to You under this Licence.

b If any provision of this Licence is invalid or unenforceable under applicable law, it shall not affect the validity or enforceability of the remainder of the terms of this Licence, and without further action by the parties to this agreement, such provision shall be reformed to the minimum extent necessary to make such provision valid and enforceable.

c No term or provision of this Licence shall be deemed waived and no breach consented to unless such waiver or consent shall be in writing and signed by the party to be charged with such waiver or consent.

d This Licence constitutes the entire agreement between the parties with respect to the Work licensed here.There are no understandings, agreements or representations with respect to the Work not specified here. Licensor shall not be bound by any additional provisions that may appear in any communication from You.This Licence may not be modified without the mutual written agreement of DEMOS and You.